On Track

A FIELD GUIDE TO SAN FRANCISCO'S
HISTORIC STREETCARS & CABLE CARS

by

RICK LAUBSCHER

Heyday, Berkeley, California
Market Street Railway, San Francisco, California

Library of Congress Cataloging-in-Publication Data

Laubscher, Rick.
On track : a field guide to San Francisco's historic streetcars and
cable cars / by Rick Laubscher.
    pages cm
ISBN 978-1-59714-278-6 (pbk. : alk. paper)
1. Street-railroads--California--San Francisco. 2. Electric
railroads--California--San Francisco. 3. Cable cars
(Streetcars)--California--San Francisco. 4. Electric
railroads--Cars--California--San Francisco. 5. San Francisco
(Calif.)--Description and travel. I. Title.
TF725.S27L38 2014
388.4'60979461--dc 3
                        2013041016

Cover Photo: Rick Laubscher
Cover and Interior Design: David Dugan
Printed in East Peoria, IL, by Versa Press, Inc.

On Track was published by Heyday
and Market Street Railway.
Orders, inquiries, and correspondence should
be addressed to:

Heyday
P.O. Box 9145, Berkeley, CA 94709
(510) 549-3564, Fax (510) 549-1889
www.heydaybooks.com

10 9 8 7 6 5 4 3 2

FOR KELSEY, KATEY, AND CAROLINE

INTRODUCTION

This book tells you about San Francisco's famed cable cars and historic streetcars, and how to use them to enjoy one of the world's great cities.

Since the cable cars and streetcars are an integrated part of the city's transit system—the San Francisco Municipal Railway (Muni)—there are always new developments to report. That's where our website, www.streetcar.org, helps you out. You can see the latest on the operating status of every vehicle in the city's historic rail fleet, view a map that shows which streetcars are on the lines, and get the latest news on these 'Museums in Motion'. You can also do all of this and more by visiting our San Francisco Railway Museum at the F-line Steuart Street stop, 77 Steuart Street, across from the Ferry Building (details are on page 127).

The proceeds from this book go to help Market Street Railway carry out its nonprofit mission of preserving historic transit in San Francisco. We invite you to join us as a member or a donor by visiting our museum or our website. Thanks.

LEARN MORE AT
streetcar.org

RIDING TIPS

1 Both the cable cars and streetcars are far less crowded in the mornings and late evenings. If you can ride before 10am or after 9pm, you'll enjoy your ride more.

2 If there are big lines at the Powell Street cable car turntables, consider riding the California line instead (p.88). It's rarely crowded and offers great views.

3 Have your fare calculated and ready before getting on the rail vehicle. This speeds boarding. Current fares will be posted on signs at each streetcar stop and at cable car terminals. As of early 2017, cash fares are:

CABLE CARS
(one way)

YOUTH & ADULT (age 5+)
$7

Under age 5 no charge.

No transfers issued or accepted. Cable car conductors can make change for up to $20 bills.

HISTORIC STREETCARS
(one way)

ADULT (age 18-64)
$2.50

YOUTH (5-17) and SENIOR (65+)
$1.25

Under age 5 no charge.

Transfers from other Muni vehicles accepted. Exact change is required on the historic streetcars!

MUNI PASSPORTS

Muni passports allow you to ride all Muni vehicles without limit, including buses, historic streetcars, and cable cars. They are priced the same for all ages.

As of early 2017, fares are:

1-DAY PASSPORT	3-DAY PASSPORT	7-DAY PASSPORT
$21	**$32**	**$42**

They are available at numerous locations, including the Powell Street Cable Car Turntable and at the San Francisco Railway Museum, 77 Steuart Street.

See more detailed tips on pages 74-75.

RIDE THE STEEL TRIANGLE

A great way to see as many historic streetcars and cable cars as possible in a short time is to travel a triangle route between Downtown, the Ferry Building, and Fisherman's Wharf, riding a cable car in one direction, a streetcar in the other.

The most scenic ride

Start aboard a Powell-Hyde cable car from Powell & Market to Hyde & Beach, giving you a look at the 'Crookedest Street' at Lombard & Hyde, and then the plunge down the Hyde Street hill to Aquatic Park as the finale. After finishing your cable car ride, walk two blocks east (away from Ghirardelli Square) on Beach Street and you'll reach the F-line terminal, where you can head to the Ferry Building and then up Market on a streetcar to reach your starting point. Once you leave the Powell turntable, this triangular trip takes about 90 minutes.

The least crowded ride

Start on an F-line streetcar at Fifth & Market (near the Powell Street cable car turntable). Ride around to the Wharf and get off at the Taylor Street stop just before the terminal (right under the giant Fisherman's Wharf sign shaped like a ship's wheel). Walk three blocks south (away from the Wharf restaurants) on Taylor Street to Bay Street and the turntable for the Powell-Mason cable car. Most times of the year, your wait for the cable car ride will be much shorter this way.

See more handy riding tips on pages 74-75.

Table of Contents

The distinct sections of this book are color-coded for quick and easy reference on the go.

Saving San Francisco's Streetcars

Rail transit has been part of San Francisco's main drag, Market Street, since 1860! But in the early 1980s, it was gravely threatened. A new subway under Market Street was opening, with modern 'light rail vehicles' that would also run on the surface at the outer end of Muni's five streetcar lines. Muni planners had proposed continuing surface streetcar service on Market, but there was little momentum and other priorities were taking precedence. The streamlined 'PCC' streetcars that had been Muni mainstays for a third of a century appeared doomed.

Then a group of civic activists (including this author, at the time a corporate communications executive and transportation committee chair of the San Francisco Chamber of Commerce) boosted the Muni planners' efforts by organizing a demonstration project called the San Francisco Historic Trolley Festival.

With the backing of the Chamber and neighborhood and business groups along Market Street, Mayor Dianne Feinstein enthusiastically approved the plan for a summer of vintage streetcar service in 1983, from Castro Street to the Financial District, using existing tracks and streetcars from Muni's own fleet as well as those leased or purchased from museums and others. (Mayor Feinstein also liked the project's potential to provide a substitute attraction for the cable cars, which were then shut down for complete rehabilitation.)

Opening Day of the first Trolley Festival, May 27, 1983. Left to right, Mayor Dianne Feinstein, Chamber of Commerce Chair Gordon Swanson, Rick Laubscher, Muni's Rino Bini.

The Trolley Festival was a big success with residents and visitors alike. People loved the variety of streetcars, the helpful operators, and the positive environment. It seemed like more than transit to them. So, it was repeated every summer for five years, proving the impetus for the permanent F-line, which opened in 1995 and was extended to Fisherman's Wharf in 2000.

During the Trolley Festival years, the primary advocacy role shifted to a nonprofit organization with a proud name: Market Street Railway. This small group of activists attracted more than 1,200 members, people who loved the idea of preserving historic transit in San Francisco.

The volunteer-led Market Street Railway has helped Muni acquire or restore more than a dozen historic streetcars from all over the world. We have successfully advocated for public funding to build the F-line, extend it, and add a second historic line, the E-Embarcadero. We tell the story of historic transit through displays, artifacts, and vintage film and photography at our San Francisco Railway Museum at the Steuart Street F-line stop across from the Ferry Building and through our website, www.streetcar.org, and our member newsletter, *Inside Track*. Our volunteers even clean the streetcars during their trips to improve riders' experiences.

F-line opening, September 1, 1995.

Today, through the continuing efforts of the people of Muni and its parent, the San Francisco Municipal Transportation Agency, and with support from Market Street Railway, the F-line is the most popular traditional streetcar line in America, its colorful cars already an icon of San Francisco.

On top of all this, we also support Muni's operation of the National Historic Landmark cable car system by enhancing the appearance and historic look of the Powell and California Street cable cars.

Market Street Railway does all this and more with no government funding—just contributions from our members and friends, plus sales of products such as this book. You can learn more, and join us, at www.streetcar.org/support.

Only in San Francisco

"San Francisco: Everyone's Favorite City." For many years, that was the official slogan of this town's convention and visitors bureau. Now the slogan is "Only in San Francisco." That's literally true when it comes to historic transit.

Only in San Francisco can you ride both the world famous cable cars and vintage electric streetcars (often called trolleys) as well. These two types of historic transit vehicles are real contributors to that 'favorite city' feeling held by so many visitors and residents.

But it could easily have turned out differently. The San Francisco you see today almost became a city you wouldn't find as appealing to live in or visit.

Envision San Francisco without its heart—the cable cars. Envision no clanging streetcars on our main drag, Market Street. Then envision a double-deck freeway on the waterfront from the Bay Bridge all the way past Fisherman's Wharf, blocking views of the bay. Picture another freeway slashing through Golden Gate Park. And a 50-story skyscraper plunked on a pier in the bay, right next to the Ferry Building.

All these things almost happened. Citizen activism stopped them.

San Franciscans are passionate about their city. They know they live in a wondrous place, one of the most spectacular urban settings on earth. They treasure their inheritance of historic buildings and green open spaces. And they fight change when they think it's not for the better.

That's why one woman, Friedel Klussmann, led a citizen revolt

Photo credit: Kevin Sheridan.

against the mayor and the city's power structure in 1947 and saved the Powell Street cable cars from replacement by buses. That's why a group of preservationists (including this writer) kept alive the tradition of rail transit on Market Street that started before the Civil War. And it's why other passionate San Franciscans turned back other threats to the city's urban fabric over the years.

Time travel

As a result, a trip to San Francisco is more than a visit to one of the world's most scenic and vibrant cities. It's also time travel, for in no other place can you ride two different types of vintage rail transit vehicles and, in the process, see such a wide variety of historic sites, intermixed with vibrant new development that reflects the ongoing evolution of the City by the Bay.

That's what this book is about. Riding history to see history.

In these pages, we'll tell the remarkable stories of San Francisco's cable cars and streetcars and describe each car so you'll know its history when you see it on the street. We'll point out historic sights to see as you ride along the routes, along with some more modern attractions. And we'll give you tips for getting the most enjoyment out of this unique transportation system, avoiding waits in line, finding the best seats, and getting off where others don't to see places often known only to long-time San Franciscans.

Also in these pages, you'll learn about the Municipal Railway (Muni), part of the San Francisco Municipal Transportation Agency, which owns and operates the cable cars and streetcars

and makes a commitment to history unmatched among public transportation agencies. You'll also learn about Market Street Railway, Muni's nonprofit preservation partner, which—while not involved with the operation of the historic vehicles—works to preserve historic transit in San Francisco.

A vintage experience

Bear in mind that riding the cable cars and vintage streetcars is hardly a luxury tour. There's no air conditioning...except for the fog. The seats don't recline—in fact, while some are upholstered, most are wood. And while on some

streetcars the ride is smooth and quiet, on others—as on the cable cars—it's often bouncy and noisy.

That's the whole point. This book carries you back to the day when what we now call historic transit was just plain transit: the way people got from here to there in cities around the world. This ride through time may be one of the most enjoyable journeys you'll ever take—and at public transit prices, it will certainly be one of the cheapest. On the way, you'll also learn how public transit played a huge role in making San Francisco the city it is today...everyone's favorite city.

So let's get started. Our time machines are waiting.

When you board one of San Francisco's world-famous cable cars, you ride along streets that have heard the click of that cable and the rumble of steel wheels on steel rails as far back as 1878. You pass architectural treasures and historic sites galore, capturing the flavor of San Francisco's past as well as its present.

Similarly, when you ride a streetcar along Market Street, you're continuing a tradition of rail service on our main drag that began before the Civil War, starting with steam trains in 1860 that gave way to horsecars, then cable cars in 1883, then electric streetcars after the great earthquake and fire of 1906.

By contrast, when you ride a streetcar along our waterfront boulevard, The Embarcadero, you're part of a new tradition begun at the turn of the 21st century. You ride mainly where streetcars never went before, passing a mix of new and historic architecture that reflects the evolution of our bayfront from one of the nation's busiest shipping ports to a vibrant mix of residential, commercial, and recreational uses.

The real deal
The vehicles themselves are part of the history, of course. No replicas or fakes here. San Francisco's vintage streetcars were built between 1896 and 1952, and Muni takes great pains to maintain their original look and feel, though consistent with modern safety and accessibility standards. Some of Muni's cable cars date back to 1888. Even the newer cable cars (they do wear out, after all) are handcrafted by Muni artisans to traditional standards.

But people often get confused between the two types of vehicles, so read on for a primer on the difference between cable cars and streetcars.

CABLE CARS run on steel rails with a slot between them. Under the slot, beneath the street, is an endless cable powered by elaborate winding machinery in a central powerhouse location. The car grabs onto the constantly-moving cable by means of a grip that acts like a giant pair of pliers, reaching through the slot underneath the street. This type of street-running cable car was invented in San Francisco in 1873 and soon spread to dozens of cities around the world, including London, Paris, Sydney, New York, Chicago, Los Angeles, Seattle, and Oakland. Though cable cars were the most advanced form of American urban rail transportation when they appeared, they were soon eclipsed by electric streetcars, and began to disappear. In 1957, San Francisco became the last remaining city in the world to operate cable cars in revenue service.

STREETCARS also run on steel rails, but have a trolley pole (or pantograph) on the roof that connects to a single overhead electric wire for power. Made practical in 1887, electric streetcars dominated urban mass transit in the U.S. until the onset of World War II. In some cities, particularly in the Eastern U.S., streetcars were known as trolleys (a term that technically refers to the wheel at the end of the pole on the roof that collects the electric current from the overhead wire; today a carbon slider is used in place of a trolley wheel). In most of the country, though, they were known as streetcars or simply cars, back in the days when what we now commonly call cars were known as automobiles, horseless carriages, or machines. In Great Britain and most countries it ruled or influenced at the time, streetcars were (and still are) called trams.

In this book, we call cable cars and streetcars by those names alone. If someone asks you where to "catch the trolley" and you want to sound like a San Franciscan, reply, "Do you mean the cable cars or the streetcars?"

☞ Now, let's look at the cars of the historic fleet one by one.

Timeline: Electric Streetcars in SF

1892—SF's first streetcar line started on Steuart Street, at site of today's San Francisco Railway Museum

1906—Market Street cable car lines converted to electric streetcars following earthquake and fire

1912—Municipal Railway (Muni), first publicly owned big city streetcar line, begins operation on Geary Street

1918—Muni opens world's longest streetcar tunnel under Twin Peaks, accelerating residential development of city's southwest quarter

1918—Market Street becomes one of world's busiest streetcar streets, with four sets of streetcar tracks running from the Ferry Building to Castro (two for Muni, two for its private competitor)

1928—Muni opens N-Judah line from Ferry Building to Ocean Beach through new Sunset Tunnel under Buena Vista Park

1932—Peak of streetcar service in San Francisco: more than 50 lines and 1,200 streetcars

1944—Muni merges with private competitor Market Street Railway Company

1948—Muni begins acquiring streamlined 'PCC' streetcars to replace old fleet

1948-56—More than two dozen streetcar lines are replaced by buses, leaving only the J, K, L, M, and N lines

1982—Last PCC streetcars retired as J, K, L, M, and N lines complete conversion to new light rail vehicles and subway operation under Market Street

1983—Vintage streetcars return to Market for successful Historic Trolley Festival, which runs five summers and leads to approval of permanent F-line

1995—F-line opens along Market Street; it is the city's first new permanent streetcar line in 63 years

2000—F-line extended to Fisherman's Wharf

2007—T-line opens, returning streetcar service to Third Street for the first time since World War II

2016—Second historic streetcar line, E-Embarcadero, starts 7-day service

San Francisco regularly operates one of the largest and most diverse fleets of vintage streetcars in the world. Muni owns more than 80 streetcars built before 1955; of these, more than 50 are currently in service or actively being restored. These are the streetcars we'll show you here. Muni's vintage streetcars broadly fall into three categories:

1. San Francisco Antiques

These are the heart of Muni's collection, irreplaceable pieces of San Francisco's heritage. Built between 1895 and 1924, they represent the heyday of the city's streetcar era, when San Francisco boasted 50 streetcar lines and more than 900 streetcars. Both passenger and work cars are part of the collection.

Find the latest status report on each of Muni's vintage streetcars at streetcar.org.

Photo credits. Top photo: David Dugan.
Bottom photos, clockwise from top right: Rick Laubscher; Bob McVay (Walter Rice collection); Rick Laubscher.

Muni's Vintage Streetcars

2. Wheels of the World

These are streetcars and trams from a variety of world cities, built between 1924 and 1952, which serve as symbols of the diversity of SF and celebrate the city's international outlook.

3. Streetcars Named Success

Most often seen on Muni's historic routes, the streamlined 'PCC' streetcars were designed in 1935 by the President's Conference Committee of U.S. electric railway leaders to bring modern looks and technology to streetcars and to meet then-growing competition from automobiles. The most successful streetcar ever built, 4,500 PCCs ran in 33 cities. They were the mainstay of San Francisco's streetcar fleet from the 1950s through the 1970s.

All three classes of Muni's vintage streetcars are authentic, not reproductions. The 'San Francisco Antiques' wear accurate liveries (exterior paint schemes) representing a specific period of their service life. The 'Wheels of the World' cars, with one exception, wear accurate liveries from their home cities. PCC streetcars ran in 33 cities in North America with only minor design variations. The streetcars in Muni's PCC fleet wear carefully researched historic liveries paying tribute to these cities. Muni's actual PCC streetcars, all built between 1946 and 1952, come from three sources: its own original PCC fleet, and used streetcars purchased from Philadelphia and from Newark, New Jersey (which in turn had acquired them from Minneapolis-St. Paul). We use the term "tribute livery" to signify that a particular PCC is painted to honor a particular city. If the page doesn't say "tribute livery," it means that streetcar actually ran in the city whose paint scheme it wears.

For up-to-the-minute information on the status of a particular streetcar or recent additions to the fleet, visit **www.streetcar.org/streetcars**.

Photo credits. Left column, from top: Jeremy Whiteman; Kevin Sheridan; Jeremy Whiteman.
Right column, from top: Jeremy Whiteman; Jeremy Whiteman.

This vehicle is easily worthy of National Historic Landmark status, or inclusion in the Smithsonian's transportation collection. It is the first publicly owned big city streetcar in American history.

Early in the 20th century, American transit systems were privately owned, often part of electric utilities. As a reaction to graft and corruption on the part of the city's privately owned streetcar company, United Railroads of San Francisco (URR), and as a reflection of the Progressive Era then sweeping California, San Franciscans passed a bond to build their own public system, the Municipal Railway, first of its kind in a major American city. Mayor James Rolph personally piloted the first Muni streetcar, No. 1, onto Geary Street on December 28, 1912. 50,000 San Franciscans turned out to celebrate.

Car No. 1 retains its original design, including woven rattan seats and maple interior trim.

builder
W.L. Holman, 1912

seats
48

weight
50,000 lb. (22,700 kg)

length
47'1" (14.4m)

width
8'6" (2.6m)

height
11'9" (3.6m)

motors
four Westinghouse 306CA

control
Westinghouse HL

trucks
two Brill 27G

brakes
Westinghouse SM Air

1912 Built in San Francisco by W. L. Holman for $7,700, part of Muni's first order of ten streetcars.

1912-51 Used in regular service, most frequently on the F-Stockton (now part of the 30-Stockton bus) and the C-California (now part of the 1-California bus) lines.

1951 Retired from daily service, motors removed, set aside for possible museum display. (All 42 other cars of this type were scrapped.)

1962 Restored to original 1912 condition by Muni shops to serve as centerpiece of Muni's 50th anniversary celebration.

1962-82 Used occasionally for charter and special service on J, K, L, M and N lines.

1983 Mayor Dianne Feinstein piloted car No. 1 down Market Street to open the first San Francisco Historic Trolley Festival.

1984-87 Operated summers in subsequent Trolley Festivals.

1995 Began serving the new F-Market line, built as a result of the Trolley Festivals.

2000 Led the parade of streetcars to open the F-line extension on The Embarcadero to Fisherman's Wharf.

2009-11 Fully restored to as-new condition to serve as centerpiece of Muni's 2012 centennial.

First trip, December 28, 1912

Bob McVay photo

Geary Street, late 1940s

Will Whittaker photo

C-line terminal, 32nd Ave., 1944

builder
Jewett Car Co., Ohio, 1914

seats
50

weight
48,000 lb. (21,800 kg)

length
47'1" (14.4m)

width
9'2" (2.8m)

height
12'3" (3.7m)

motors
four Westinghouse 532A

control
Westinghouse HL

trucks
Baldwin L-plate

brakes
Westinghouse SME Air

This car was one of Muni's workhouses for 44 years, but is lucky to be here today. Built in 1914, part of an order of 125 cars to expand Muni service for the Panama-Pacific International Exposition in the Marina District, car No. 130 operated on almost every Muni streetcar line during its initial career.

Car No. 130 was the last Iron Monster to leave passenger service, in 1958. Muni shop foreman Charlie Smallwood saved it from the scrap heap by hiding it in the back of the Geneva car house while its mates met their fates. He then talked his bosses into making it a wrecker. Stripped bare and painted yellow, it spent the next 25 years towing its replacements (PCC streetcars) back to the barn when they broke down. It was fully restored by Muni craftsworkers in 1983 for the Historic Trolley Festival. Charlie had kept the original seats all those years in his basement … just in case! The saga of this car has inspired a children's book, *Lucky 130* by Mae Silver.

1914 Built for Muni in Ohio by Jewett Car Co.

1914-58 Used in regular service on virtually every Muni streetcar line. Painted in all three Muni liveries used during its service life, including the green and cream 'Wings' in the 1950s.

1958 Retired from daily service. Seats removed, equipment installed to allow car to serve as Geneva Division wrecker. (Only two of the 125 cars of this type survive. Market Street Railway acquired car No. 162 from Orange Empire Railway Museum in Southern California in 2002 and gifted it to Muni.)

1983 Restored by Muni craftsworkers to 1939 appearance with blue and gold paint (pictured at top) to participate in San Francisco Historic Trolley Festival.

1984-87 Operated summers in subsequent Trolley Festivals.

1995 Begins serving F-Market line, built as result of successful Trolley Festivals.

2000 Begins serving F-line extension on The Embarcadero to Fisherman's Wharf.

Converted to a wrecker, 1960s

Richard Panse photo

On F-line

This is almost certainly the last original Muni streetcar to 'come home' to operate again in San Francisco. It was reacquired in 2003 by the nonprofit Market Street Railway and Muni from the Orange Empire Railway Museum in Riverside County.

Market Street Railway volunteers replaced the roof canvas and made a number of body repairs to the car. It then went to Muni's shops in 2004, where master craftsworkers finished the meticulous restoration in 2008.

This car is painted in its last Muni livery, the Postwar 'Wings' introduced at the end of the 1940s and kept until the retirement of the car in 1958. Like its twin, preserved car No. 130 (in 1939 blue and gold livery), this car ran on virtually all of Muni's streetcar lines, spending much time on the H-line along Van Ness and Potrero Avenues and through Fort Mason. Like No. 130, its large size and long-term reliability makes it a workhorse of the historic fleet, and very popular with San Franciscans of the Boomer Generation who remember it from childhood.

1914 Built for Muni in Ohio by Jewett Car Company, part of same order as car No. 130.

1914-58 Used in regular service on virtually every Muni streetcar line. Painted in all three Muni liveries used during its service life, including the green and cream 'Wings' in the 1950s.

1958 Retired from daily service. Sold to Orange Empire Railway Museum in Southern California.

2003 Repurchased by Market Street Railway and Muni and returned to San Francisco, where Market Street Railway volunteers began cosmetic restoration of the car.

2004 Moved to Green Division, in part under its own power, for further work by Muni, including modern electronic package, in preparation for revenue service.

2008 Reenters Muni service after 50-year 'vacation'.

builder
Jewett Car Co., Ohio, 1914

seats
46

weight
48,000 lb. (21,800 kg)

length
47'1" (14.4m)

width
9'2" (2.8m)

height
12'3" (3.7m)

motors
four Westinghouse 532A

control
Westinghouse HL

trucks
Baldwin L-plate

brakes
Westinghouse SME Air

Jim Lekas photo

On M-Ocean View line, 1957

David Dugan photo

On F-line

builder
Hammond Car Co., 1896

seats
26

weight
20,300 lb. (9,200 kg)

length
26'2" (8.0m)

width
8'0" (2.4m)

height
11'6" (3.5m)

motors
two G.E. 1000

control
K

trucks
Peckham single

brakes
hand

San Francisco streetcar No. 578 may be the world's oldest streetcar still on the active roster of an urban transit agency.

Built in 1896 by the same firm that later built the California Street cable cars, this historic treasure, a bouncy single-trucker, was part of San Francisco's first generation of electric streetcars. It survived the 1906 cataclysm and then dodged the scrapper's torch by being converted into a work car.

In 1956, Muni craftsworkers beautifully restored it to its original appearance as part of the 50th anniversary commemoration of the earthquake and fire. It was later put on 'permanent loan' to a rail museum, on the belief that Muni would not use it again. But the Historic Trolley Festivals led to its recall to active Muni service.

Though operational, it is only rarely used in revenue service, given its size and age. The outside seats were slightly shortened in 2004 to allow wheelchair accessibility. Plans have been discussed to fit it with a track brake used on many cars of this class.

1896 Built in San Francisco by Hammond Car Company for the original Market Street Railway Company. Operated primarily in Western Addition and Downtown.

post-1906 Converted into a sand car (work equipment) for Geneva Division; acquired by Muni in 1944 as part of its purchase of Market Street Railway Company.

1956 Restored by Muni craftsworkers for earthquake 50th anniversary service, later loaned to museum in Solano County.

1984 Recalled by Muni for Trolley Festival service; used for E-line demonstration on Embarcadero freight tracks in 1987.

1995 After F-line startup, used occasionally in special service, including 'preview' E-line service in 2001 (pictured at right).

2004 Seats in end section slightly shortened to accommodate wheelchairs.

At Pier 39

Demonstration service on E-line

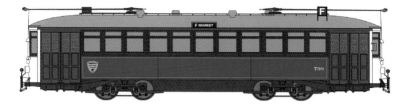

The land at Ocean and San Jose Avenues, next to today's BART Balboa Park Station, has housed streetcar repair facilities for more than a century. Muni's Curtis E. Green Light Rail Division now occupies the site. Between 1923 and 1933, though, craftsworkers from the old Market Street Railway Co. hand-built some 250 streetcars on this site, at the now-vanished Elkton Shops.

Car No. 798 is the only one of these home-built streetcars left.

Built in 1924, old photographs show it running on the 19-Polk, 27-Bryant, 35-Howard, and 11-Mission and 24th St. lines, operating out of the car house at 24th and Utah Streets. Retired just after World War II, the body became a store in the Sierra Nevada foothills. It was saved from destruction in 1984 through private donations and presented to Muni, which invested more than $300,000 to have the body restored at a Tracy prison. But the project stalled, and No. 798 eventually started to deteriorate at the Geneva Division. Market Street Railway volunteers restored the body again. Funding is being sought to complete the mechanical and electrical restoration of the streetcar. This sole survivor of its class will take a place of pride on Muni's tracks when restoration is complete.

1924 Built by Market Street Railway Company craftsworkers at Elkton Shops.

1946 Retired by Muni (acquired with the Market Street Railway Co. assets in 1944) and sold; body ultimately moved to Columbia, California, becoming a jewelry store.

1984 Threatened with destruction, car No. 798 body acquired for Muni through private donations; moved by Hetch Hetchy crews to San Francisco.

1989 No. 798 moved to state prison in Tracy, where prisoners rebuilt body under contract to Muni.

2001 Untouched since prison work, deteriorated body of No. 798 is restored again by Market Street Railway volunteers, who also install seats and other components to prepare car for final electrical and mechanical work by Muni.

builder
Market Street Railway Co., San Francisco, 1924

seats
50

weight
39,895 lb. (18,100 kg)

length
47′0″ (14.3m)

width
8′9″ (2.7m)

height
12′0″ (3.7m)

original motors
four G.E. 1000

original control
K 12

original trucks
Brill 27G

brakes
air

On 11-line at Ferry Building, 1930s

Karl Johnson photo

Being restored by Market St. Railway

builder
Pacific Car and Equipment Co.,
South San Francisco, 1916

weight
40,000 lb. (21,800 kg)

length
40'8" (14.4m)

width
8'6" (2.8m)

bin capacity
20 cubic yards

motors
four Westinghouse 306CA

control
Westinghouse HL

trucks
Brill (34" wheels)

When electric streetcars came along, they took over from horse cars in many cities. This streetcar did the work of horses in a different way. Muni streetcar No. C-1 wasn't built to carry passengers. Properly called a *motor flat*, it was built to carry almost everything else, though.

In the early 20th century, streetcar tracks often ran on unpaved streets, and well away from the city centers to what was then the country. Streetcar operators needed a variety of work equipment to keep the tracks and overhead wires in shape and perform odd jobs. Most operators around the country converted obsolete passenger cars to do these often-dirty tasks. But Muni's first work car was specially built to…well, work!

This car was built new, to Muni's specifications, by Pacific Car and Equipment Co. of South San Francisco in 1916. As the decades went by, C-1 was used less frequently as rubber-tired service trucks proved more flexible for most maintenance jobs.

In early 1992, Muni needed a test car with the same wheelbase as the new Breda LRVs on order. They wanted to ensure that the new cars, as designed, would clear all the tight spots on the system. So they recalled No. C-1 and fit it with a framework that matched the body dimensions of the Breda cars. Then, with contributions from Breda and help from Muni, Market Street Railway volunteers restored the car, by now considerably altered, to its original appearance as a gift to Muni for its 80th birthday, fabricating new drop sides to replace long-gone originals, stripping and varnishing the oak sash and door, and creating a fresh gold-leaf "MR" logo, a handsome insignia that Muni surprisingly applied to only this car.

The motor flat's return to active duty was officially celebrated on Muni's 80th birthday, December 28, 1992. Carefully tended by Market Street Railway and Muni, it remains a blue-collar car, now fitted with a generator that frees it from needing overhead wires. Its most frequent job in the last decade has been testing new track and switches installed as part of the reconstruction of existing lines, and the creation of new ones, such as the F-line and the T-line.

Though it doesn't carry passengers, it still carries a place of honor in Muni's historic streetcar fleet.

When new, 1916

Steve Ferrario photo

Testing new track on N-line

Originally built for:
Porto, Portugal, 1929.

Acquired by Muni from:
Paul Class, Oregon, 1984.

The J.G. Brill Co. of Philadelphia was one of the greatest streetcar builders in the world. Its products ran all over the world, and one city that depended on Brill streetcars for more than half a century was Porto, Portugal.

Car No. 189 is actually a copy of the famous Brill design, built by Porto's own streetcar shops in 1929. Both Porto and Lisbon ran Brill trolleys (and locally produced copies) throughout the 20th century. Lisbon has lovingly restored and updated a few of its lines, and Porto, too, has retained a vintage line that still uses these cars.

But some of Porto's old Brills—both tiny single-truck cars and somewhat larger (but still small) double-truckers—got scattered across the globe when the city cut lines in the 1980s. They were perfect for heritage trolley operations, since they were similar to streetcars that had run in many American cities (though, interestingly enough, never in San Francisco).

When the first San Francisco Historic Trolley Festival was planned in 1983, the Chamber of Commerce leased two ex-Porto single-truck cars from Paul Class, an Oregon streetcar entrepreneur. Their bouncy ride, beautiful interior woodwork and rattan seats made them very popular. But the cars were very tired mechanically, and their wood bodies were held together more by inertia than anything else. Since the Festival was originally conceived as a one-time event, these cars were not intended to have a permanent home here. Indeed, one of the cars, No. 122 (a 1912 Brill kit), went to Dallas, where it operates today as part of the delightful McKinney Avenue heritage trolley line.

This car, No. 189, was brought back to San Francisco in 1984, bought by Muni, and operated in the remainder of the Trolley Festivals. In 1987, it joined the only other single-truck car in the fleet (No. 578) in a successful demonstration of the potential popularity of a waterfront streetcar line…a trial run that clinched the extension of the F-line along the waterfront to Fisherman's Wharf.

Car No. 189 currently awaits restoration.

builder
Porto, Portugal, 1929

seats
22

weight
28,000 lb. (12,700 kg)

length
30'6" (9.3m)

width
7'6" (2.3m)

height
11'3" (3.4m)

motors
two

control
G.E. K with electric brake

trucks
air, electric, hand

Jim Lekas photo

On Market during Trolley Fest., 1983

David Dugan photo

Ornate interior

builder
English Electric, 1934

seats
44

weight
20,000 lb. (9,100 kg)

length
42'3" (12.9m)

width
7'6" (2.3m)

height
10'3" (3.1m)
excluding trolley tower

motors
two English Electric 305

control
BTH B18 (No. 228)
English Electric Z-type (No. 233)

trucks
English Electric

brakes
air, self-lapping, hand

Kevin Sheridan photo

No. 228 at Ferry Building

No. 233 arrives in California, 2013

Identical tram in Blackpool, UK

Originally built for:
Blackpool Tramways, Blackpool, England, 1934.

No. 228 acquired by Muni from:
Blackpool Tramways, Blackpool, England, 1984.

No. 233 bought by Market Street Ry. for Muni from:
Lancastrian Transport Trust, Blackpool, England, 2013.

One of the most unusual streetcar types ever built comes from Blackpool, England's venerable seaside resort. Twelve of these open-top, canoe-shaped trams were built for that city in 1934, and now, thanks to Market Street Railway, San Francisco has two of them.

For many years, boat trams ran on good weather days along the coastal promenade, sharing the tracks with a wide variety of unusual English-built equipment. In the fall, Blackpool trams are specially decorated for the 'illuminations', with elaborate lighting making the cars sparkle as the sun sets over the Irish Sea.

Muni leased boat tram No. 226 from a museum for the early Trolley Festivals. Then, Market Street Railway members went after one that Muni could own, and struck gold with boat tram No. 228, which had already crossed the Atlantic in 1976 to delight Philadelphians as part of that city's bicentennial celebration. Returned to Blackpool, it sat unused until Blackpool donated it to San Francisco as a gesture of friendship. Muni craftsworkers restored the car to its Blackpool look.

Because No. 228 brought so much delight to thousands of riders in San Francisco, Market Street Railway waited patiently for years for another of the rare boat trams to become available. In 2013, it found success when the Lancastrian Transport Trust, a preservation group in Blackpool, determined it would sell the boat tram it owned (No. 233) to help fund repairs to an older double-deck Blackpool tram. Blackpool itself still operates three boat trams, and now San Francisco has two, increasing the opportunity for riders on our waterfront to hear the same tooting air whistle as they do on the Irish seacoast…and enjoy a boat cruise on the land!

No. 233's acquisition was funded through a generous grant from the Thoresen Foundation, with shipping arranged and underwritten by FedEx Trade Networks. No. 228 was shipped to San Francisco thanks to support from Bechtel Group.

Originally built for:

Johnstown Traction Co., Johnstown, Pennsylvania, 1926.

Acquired by Muni from:

Mrs. Herb Redlich, Freestone, California, late 1980s.

While this historic streetcar has not yet operated on San Francisco's streets, it is included here because of the value it could bring to future generations.

Muni's erstwhile competitor, Market Street Railway Company, dedicated a special streetcar to taking San Francisco school kids on field trips in the 1920s and 1930s. That car is still remembered today as the private company's most successful public relations tool. Today's nonprofit Market Street Railway purchased a vintage streetcar from a private party in the Bay Area with the idea of reviving this tradition: a 'Teaching Trolley' that would mostly run in regular service as part of the core historic fleet, but would be outfitted with teaching aids for school classes and other groups to charter, and to attract families to the city on weekends and in summers.

Car No. 351 itself is a classic American trolley: a 1926 double-end, arch-roof steel car from Johnstown, Pennsylvania, of a design virtually identical to cars once operated by the old Market Street Railway Company. It is complete with original rattan seats and wood trim and has received protective preservation by the nonprofit Market Street Railway, which intends to donate the car to Muni once restoration plans have been agreed on. These plans, if realized, could revive an old San Francisco tradition and teach students and their families the value of attractive public transit in building great cities.

builder
St. Louis Car Co., 1926

seats
44

weight
36,680 lb. (16,640 kg)

length
41'5" (12.6m)

width
7'0" (2.1m)

height
11'3" (3.4m)

motors
four 35-HP Westinghouse 510A2

control
G.E. K-35KK

trucks
St. Louis Car EDJ-64

brakes
air

In Johnstown, 1944

At MSR restoration facility

25

builder
Moore, 1928

seats
52

weight
35,000 lb. (15,900 kg)

length
48'0" (14.6m)

width
9'0" (2.7m)

height
10'7" (3.2m)

motors
four General Electric

control
General Electric K35JJ

trucks
two M&MTB Type 1

brakes
air, self-lapping

L.B.
UM 2A

Originally built for:
Melbourne & Metropolitan Tramways Board (M&MTB), Melbourne, Australia, 1928.

Acquired by Muni from:
M&MTB, Melbourne, Australia, 1983.

No Southern Hemisphere city has a tram (streetcar) system as extensive as that of Melbourne, capital of Australia's State of Victoria.

Like San Francisco, Melbourne had both cable cars and streetcars well into the 20th century, but by the 1920s, the remaining cable car lines gave way to more tram lines. For half a century, Melbourne's transit system was dominated by the famed W-class trams, with a layout that reversed San Francisco's 'California' design, by putting closed sections at both ends, with the lowered section for boarding and alighting placed in the middle. This also served as the smoking section. More than 750 W-class trams were built to this general design between 1923 and 1956. Melbourne No. 496 went into service August 18, 1928.

In the late 1970s, modern trams finally began replacing the old W-class cars. In 1984, Muni purchased No. 496 (along with No. 586, kept as a spare). The tram's smooth ride made it an immediate hit in San Francisco. With volunteer help from Market Street Railway, No. 496 has been cosmetically restored, made wheelchair-accessible, and given a GPS system. Otherwise, it's essentially unchanged from its 56 years of service in Australia.

Melbourne still runs a limited number of W-class trams, primarily on its special City Centre loop line around downtown. They are now recognized as a key part of the city's heritage, much as San Francisco's cable cars and historic streetcars are.

A W2-class tram in Melbourne

Richard Panse photo

On F-line

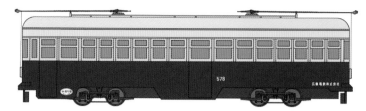

Originally built for:
Kobe City Railway, Kobe, Japan, 1927.

Acquired by Muni from:
Hiroshima Electric Railway Co., Hiroshima, Japan, 1986.

This car represents a typical Japanese tram design of the 1920s. It was built in 1927 (as car No. 574) for the Kobe City Railway. As originally built, it had single doors at each end and double doors in the center, all manually operated, but in a 1958 renovation, the rear doors (in Japan's left-hand operation) were removed. During this renovation, tram No. 574 was renumbered No. 578. The tram was renovated again in 1968 so that it could be operated by only one person, eliminating the traditional conductor. Modern touches for the day, such as a public address system, were also added.

When Kobe closed its street railways in 1971, this car was acquired by the Hiroshima Electric Railway Company and ran in passenger service using the same Kobe two-tone green livery until it came to San Francisco.

The late Maurice Klebolt, longtime Market Street Railway director, worked with Japan's Corporate Railway Assembly, an industry trade group, to bring No. 578-J to San Francisco just in time to lead the opening parade of the 1986 Trolley Festival, with Mayor Dianne Feinstein at the controls.

What was a front-and-center door tram in Japan instantly became a center-and-rear door tram in right-hand-driving America. Its two motors, perfectly adequate for the flat terrain of the Japanese cities it had served, make it somewhat slow for San Francisco service. Additionally, the tram lacked a hand brake, which became a California requirement after the Trolley Festivals concluded. Thus, No. 578-J was taken out of service for an extended period. But a hand brake has now been installed and other improvements have been made, bringing this Japanese car closer to a return to San Francisco service.

builder
Fujinagata Zosen Co., 1927

seats
36

weight
32,000 lb. (14,510 kg)

length
44'9" (13.6m)

width
8'2" (2.5m)

height
10'1" (3.1m)

motors
two 35-HP

control
British Thompson Houston

trucks
Brill 77-E

brakes
dynamic, air, hand

Sister tram No. 582, in Hiroshima

No. 578-J in Dolores Park, 1992

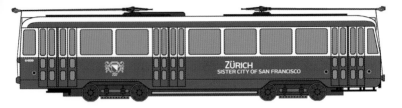

ZÜRICH
SISTER CITY OF SAN FRANCISCO

builder
La Brugeoise, Belgium, 1952

seats
33

weight
36,300 lb. (16,500 kg)

length
45'7" (13.9m)

width
7'3" (2.2m)

height
10'1" (3.0m)

motors
four Westinghouse 1432

control
Westinghouse PCC type

trucks
PCC type

Being shipped from Brussels to SF

Steve Ferrario photo

Testing on J-line

Originally built for:
Brussels, Belgium, 1952.

Acquired by Muni from:
Brussels, Belgium, 2004.

The PCC streetcar was a distinctly American invention, dreamed up by a group of transit company presidents in the early 1930s to replace old-fashioned trolleys and staunch the defection of transit riders to automobiles. After World War II, the PCC waned in America, as most transit systems converted to buses. But in that same time period, the PCC was beginning a somewhat unlikely renaissance in Europe.

The War devastated the tram (streetcar) systems of many European cities. Even those that survived unscathed found themselves with antiquated equipment, usually a tiny motor-and-trailer pair that were inefficient, drafty, and increasingly expensive to maintain. Brussels tackled this challenge in 1951 by licensing PCC technology from the United States. La Brugeoise of Brugge, Belgium, used new Westinghouse PCC motors and controls to build the first fifty PCC trams for Brussels, including this one. The body style was an amalgam of the PCC design and emerging European tram design: three sets of doors made loading and unloading faster, and the very slender profile (almost two feet narrower than Muni's widest PCCs) allowed it to snake through the tight spaces of old European cities.

The car design proved popular, and Brussels ordered hundreds more over the years. This western European design, with some variations, also operated in a number of other Belgian, French and Dutch cities. On the other side of the Iron Curtain, the PCC design was adapted by Czechoslovakia's TATRA, which churned out thousands of trams based on this U.S. technology for dozens of Soviet-bloc cities—invariably painted red.

In June 2005, No. 737 made its first appearance on San Francisco streets wearing the blue and white livery of Zürich, Switzerland, which operated similar-looking cars (but narrow gauge and non-PCC). The car temporarily wears this livery in tribute to the sister-city relationship between Zürich and San Francisco. In the future, No. 737 may be restored to its original 1952 cream Brussels livery.

New Orleans, Louisiana
Built 1923

Originally built for:

New Orleans Public Service, Inc., New Orleans, LA, 1923.

Acquired by Muni from:

952: New Orleans Regional Transit Authority, 1998.

913: Orange Empire Railway Museum, Perris, CA, 2005.

The most iconic transit vehicle in American literary history is Tennessee Williams' 'Streetcar Named Desire' from New Orleans. Muni currently has two such icons.

Car No. 952 came from New Orleans to San Francisco in 1998 by arrangement between mayors Willie Brown (San Francisco) and Marc Morial (New Orleans). The occasion was the world premier of Andre Previn's opera of Williams' novel. While the original intention of the mayors was to convey title of No. 952 to San Francisco, Louisiana state historic preservation officials required that the car be leased instead.

Car No. 952 has proven extremely popular with San Franciscans and visitors, bringing a bit of the flavor of the Crescent City to the City by the Bay and serving as an ambassador on wheels for New Orleans, with displays inside the car celebrating streetcars in New Orleans literature.

Spurred by the desire for a 'Desire' that Muni could own outright, the nonprofit Market Street Railway canvassed rail museums with New Orleans cars that had once served lines like Desire and Canal Streets and found the Orange Empire Railway Museum in Riverside County willing to sell their car No. 913, identical to No. 952, in very good and unaltered condition.

Car No. 913 was purchased for $200,000 and is awaiting restoration. It ran onto the shipping trailer under its own power. Tragically, the very day it arrived in San Francisco in 2005, its former New Orleans home was being pummeled by Hurricane Katrina. The remaining vintage cars in New Orleans, twins of Nos. 913 and 952, escaped damage, but the new replica cars on the restored Canal Street line were destroyed.

builder
Perley Thomas Co., High Point, NC, 1923

seats
54

weight
42,000 lb. (19,100 kg)

length
47'8" (14.5m)

width
8'7" (2.6m)

height
11'6" (3.5m)

motors
two G.E. 263

control
K-36

trucks
Brill 76E2

brakes
air

No. 913 on Magazine line,
Audubon Park, New Orleans, 1940s

David Dugan photo

No. 952 on F-line

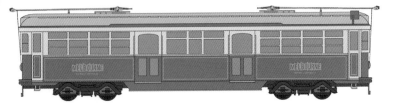

builder
Melbourne & Metropolitan
Tramways Board, 1946

seats
52

weight
38,580 lb. (17,500 kg)

length
46'6" (14.2m)

width
9'0" (2.7m)

height
10'4" (3.1m)

motors
four G.E. 247 AX2 30kW

control
M&MTB RC2

trucks
two M&MTB Type 15

brakes
air, self-lapping

Originally built for:
Melbourne & Metropolitan Tramways Board (M&MTB),
Melbourne, Australia, 1946.

Acquired by Muni from:
State Government of Victoria, Australia, 2009.

Few cities in the world have shown as much loyalty to a single streetcar design as has Melbourne. The 'W' class of trams was introduced in 1923, with a design that was the opposite of the 'California type' streetcar common on this side of the Pacific.

The Melbourne design featured entrances at the center of the car, in an open section, flanked by closed sections on each end. This design evolved over more than 40 years, with repeated rounds of modifications made to improve the design.

The last W-class car was built in 1956, numbered 1040 (coincidentally, the same number as the last PCC streetcar built in North America, for Muni).

Tram No. 916, of the 'SW6' subclass, entered service in Melbourne on June 21, 1946. The most visible advance over the earlier W-class designs (such as Muni's W2 tram No. 496) was the installation of sliding doors in the center section, keeping the car far warmer in winter (Melbourne's climate is similar to San Francisco's).

Beginning in 1975, Melbourne began replacing older W-class trams with modern designs based on contemporary European designs. Yet some of the newer W-class trams still operate in Melbourne, primarily on the free City Circle line.

This tram was donated to the City of San Francisco by the State Government of Victoria (of which Melbourne is the capital) in 2009. In exchange for the donation, Nos. 916 and 496 both carry Melbourne logos on their sides and tourism materials inside.

The donation of No. 916 was initiated and facilitated by the nonprofit Market Street Railway.

An SW6 at South Melbourne Beach

Jeremy Whiteman photo

No. 916 on T-line, 2013

The second most common type of streetcar in Muni's historic fleet is an American classic with an Italian accent. This type of car is named for Cleveland street railway commissioner Peter Witt, who designed it for his Ohio city around 1915. The concept was to speed loading by putting the conductor in the middle of the car, letting crowds board through the front door and paying as they passed the conductor.

'Peter Witts' ran in fifteen U.S. cities, including New York, Chicago, Dallas, Philadelphia, Detroit, and Los Angeles (though not, in that era, in San Francisco). The design was also exported to world cities such as Toronto, Mexico City, Madrid, and three Italian cities, Naples, Turin, and Milan.

Milan has the longest-serving Peter Witts in the world, building some 500 starting in 1928, some of which still operate today. The first Peter Witts in Milan were painted an attractive yellow and white, which changed by the early 1930s to a two-tone green livery. In the 1970s, the Milan tram fleet was painted solid orange, the livery they still wear today in the Italian city. They long ago stopped using conductors.

In 1984, one Milan tram came to San Francisco for the summer Trolley Festivals that led to construction of the F-line. It proved so reliable that Muni obtained ten more in 1998 to meet the huge F-line rider demand. Over the years, Muni has systematically upgraded these trams with modern GPS navigation and other improvements, and started a program of repainting some of the trams into authentic Milan liveries of decades past, adding even more Italian flavor to its vintage fleet.

1928 (yellow) livery
Nos. 1807, 1811

1930s (green) livery
Nos. 1814, 1818, 1888

1970s (orange) livery
Nos. 1815, 1834, 1856, 1859, 1893, 1895

builder
Carminati & Toselli, Italy, 1928

weight
33,000 lb. (14,970 kg)

length
45'7" (13.9m)

width
7'9" (2.4m)

height
12'2" (3.7m)

motors
four Milano type 2B, 21kw each

control
General Electric Italia K35

trucks
ATM Milano

brakes
air

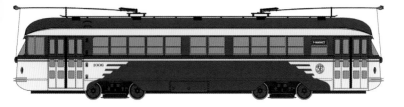

builder
St. Louis Car Co., 1948

modifier
Brookville Equipment Co., 2011

seats
60

weight
40,100 lb. (18,200 kg)

length
50'5" (15.4m)

width
9'0" (2.7m)

height
10'1" (3.1m)

motors
four General Electric 1220E1

control
General Electric

trucks
St. Louis B-3

brakes
Westinghouse electric

Kris Longa photo

At Steuart & Mission Streets

Built in 1948 for San Francisco Municipal Railway. Served San Francisco from 1948-present. Painted in original San Francisco Muni livery.

When the Presidents' Conference Committee (PCC) of U.S. street railway executives got together in the early 1930s to design a better streetcar, they wanted to get away from the boxy double-ended streetcars that then ruled the streets. So, they created a streamlined, single-end design that was more automotive in look, although it required streetcar companies to install loop tracks or switches in the shape of a "Y" to turn the cars around at the ends of lines. Almost all transit companies that could afford new streetcars embraced the sleek single-end PCC design.

Not everyone, though. The San Francisco Municipal Railway required that its first two orders of streamlined streetcars be double-ended: the five so-called 'Magic Carpet' cars of 1939 (PCC-lookalikes with different operating systems, whose livery is modeled by car No. 1010 today); and the ten true PCC-equipped streamliners delivered to Muni in 1948.

The 1948 PCCs, numbered from 1006 to 1015, were known at Muni as 'Torpedoes' because of their shape. (Later on, they were also called the 'Big Tens' to distinguish them from the 25 smaller single-end PCCs, numbered from 1016 to 1040, which were purchased in 1951-52 and were known as the 'Baby Tens'.)

The Big Tens were among the largest PCC streetcars ever built, exceeded in length only by Chicago's single-end behemoths. They were delivered in what was then a brand-new livery for Muni: green bodies with cream trim, with what resembled feathers of cream extending toward the center of the car from each door. This was quickly dubbed the 'Wings' livery, and it was applied to every Muni streetcar and bus by about 1950. The mystery of Muni's insistence on double-ended PCCs was deepened by the fact that initially they only served lines that already had loops, making double-end cars unnecessary. By the mid-1950s, Muni converted its 15 double-end streamliners to operate as single-enders by sealing the doors on one side. Around this time, these cars were painted to match the single-end PCCs, with the Wings only on the now-front end.

This car, No. 1006, was the first of the class to be delivered. It operated through the end of original Muni PCC service in 1982, and was then reconverted to a double-end car for service in the Trolley Festivals of the mid-1980s and restored to the original Wings livery it still wears today.

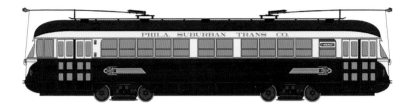

Built in 1948 for San Francisco Municipal Railway.
Served San Francisco from 1948-present.
Painted in tribute to Philadephia Suburban.

This car commemorates Philadelphia Suburban Transportation Co. (PST)—the 'Red Arrow' lines serving Philly's western suburbs—which ran interurban cars with some PCC features from 1949 to 1982.

PST's city cousin was named Philadelphia Rapid Transit (PRT) (represented by PCCs Nos. 1055 and 1060), but actually PST was far faster, running on suburban rights-of-way far from city streets.

In 1940, PST modernized its fleet with ten 'Brilliners', a PCC competitor from old-line trolley builder J.G. Brill & Co. But the PST order turned out to be the last cars Brill ever built. Needing more cars after the war, PST turned to St. Louis Car Co., which offered a body shell nearly identical to one bought by Muni (including car No. 1007) and Illinois Terminal Railroad. The Red Arrow cars, though, had rear doors only half as wide as the standard double-end body.

The 14 Red Arrow cars, delivered in 1949, were equipped with non-PCC trucks (wheel and axle assemblies), along with motors and brakes designed for fast open-track running. The PST cars were capable of reaching 70 mph. Initially, these PCC-lookalikes ran on the 19-mile West Chester line, but later served the Sharon Hill and Media lines. They had couplers and sometimes ran in two-car trains.

The private PST was taken over by the public SEPTA agency in 1970, and by 1982 the PCCs and Brilliners were supplanted by Kawasaki light rail vehicles.

Underneath the Red Arrow livery, No. 1007 itself has actually been a San Francisco Muni streetcar all its life. It ran from 1948 until 1982 on Muni's J, K, L, M, and N lines, and was then retired and stored before being rehabilitated for the F-line opening in 1995.

At first, the restored No. 1007 was painted in a modernistic silver and red San Francisco scheme like that of Muni's Breda LRVs. It wasn't popular, so Muni's paint shop applied the handsome Red Arrow livery in 1997 to honor Philadelphia Suburban Transportation Company.

builder
St. Louis Car Co., 1948

modifier
Morrison-Knudsen, 1995

seats
60

weight
40,100 lb. (18,200 kg)

length
50'5" (15.4m)

width
9'0" (2.7m)

height
10'1" (3.1m)

motors
four G.E. 1220E1

control
G.E.

trucks
St. Louis B-3

brakes
Westinghouse electric

Peter Ehrlich photo

In the new Muni livery it wore when the F-line opened

David Dugan photo

In its Red Arrow livery

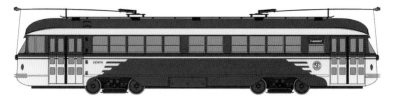

builder
St. Louis Car Co., 1948

modifier
Brookville Equipment Co., 2011

seats
60

weight
40,100 lb. (18,200 kg)

length
50'5" (15.4m)

width
9'0" (2.7m)

height
10'1" (3.1m)

motors
four General Electric 1220E1

control
General Electric

trucks
St. Louis B-3

brakes
Westinghouse electric

Todd Lappin photo

As a repair car, before restoration

Rick Laubscher photo

Fully restored

**Built in 1948 for San Francisco Municipal Railway.
Served San Francisco from 1948-present.
Painted in original San Francisco Muni livery.**

Like all of the double-end PCCs in the fleet, No. 1008 was an original Muni streetcar, and, like No. 1006, it is painted in its 'as-delivered' 1948 'Wings' livery, perhaps the best-liked Muni paint scheme ever.

Its logo, with a large S.F. ringed by the words "Municipal Railway", was designed by Michael M. O'Shaughnessy, the city's chief engineer, responsible for such projects as the 1918 Twin Peaks Tunnel that still carries Muni's rail cars under the ridge that bisects the city. He also built the system that brings San Francisco its drinking water from Yosemite.

The 'Torpedoes' of the 1006-1015 class could operate anywhere on Muni's streetcar system of the late 1940s, and right after delivery, railfans pounced on them for some special rides, such as on the original F-line along Stockton, Columbus, North Point, and Chestnut Streets (through the Stockton Tunnel, another O'Shaughnessy creation).

In regular service, the Torpedoes were usually seen on the N-Judah in their early years, never on the lines that then required double-end streetcars, such as the J-Church and the M-Ocean View.

After Muni acquired single-end PCC streetcars in the 1950s, the Torpedoes were converted to operate in service from only one end as well. But the operator's cab in what had become the rear end was largely left intact to facilitate back-up moves in the yard and on the 'wye' reversing tracks that had been installed at the ends of the J and M lines. This seat was at a high premium with young railfans, who could look through the windshield and pretend they were motormen (as long as they could get over going backward).

Strangely enough, once the J-line was converted to single-end operation, the Torpedoes became familiar sights there, even though their long wheelbase made for a tight fit on the twisty right-of-way over Dolores Heights.

When Muni ceased its original PCC service in 1982, dozens of the streamlined cars, including all eight of the surviving ten Torpedoes, were saved for future restoration. No. 1008, though, had already been serving as a test car for the tracks and wiring in then-new Muni Metro subway, and was then converted into a work car, towing broken-down streetcars back to the barn. It deteriorated over the years to a derelict state, but is now fully restored as a passenger car, its clock turned back to 1948.

Built in 1948 for San Francisco Municipal Railway.
Served San Francisco from 1948-present.
Painted in tribute to Dallas Railway & Terminal Co.

This streetcar is painted to honor Dallas, which ran PCCs from 1945 to 1956.

Dallas Railway & Terminal Company's 25 double-enders were built by Pullman-Standard and had narrower rear doors and a narrower body than Muni's Torpedoes, built by St. Louis Car Company. As Dallas' first (and last) modern streetcars, their PCCs were dubbed 'Gliding Beauties', and ran on a variety of routes around 'Big D' during their short lives there, often alongside conventional older streetcars.

Like other southern streetcar systems of that era, Dallas PCC's were segregated, with moveable signs to separate the black and white sections, blacks in the rear. (The irony, of course, was that on a double-end car, seats occupied by blacks would be occupied by whites on the return trip and vice versa.)

Dallas' PCCs arrived from the factory in a predominantly red livery with cream and silver trim. Dallas Railway & Terminal picked the colors but apparently didn't tell the builder how to apply them, so Pullman-Standard used the diagrams for its earlier Pacific Electric PCCs as a guide. This original livery, worn by No. 1009 lasted just a few years, replaced by a mostly cream livery with red trim. When Dallas retired its PCCs, they tried to sell them to other streetcar operators. New Orleans Public Service apparently considered them for its Canal and St. Charles lines, but ultimately rejected them because the narrow rear doors of the Pullman design would slow passenger flow too much.

Dallas also approached the San Francisco Municipal Railway to buy the cars, but Muni had no money for purchases at the time. (Muni ended up leasing 70 used streetcars from St. Louis Public Service in 1957 to get around this cash crunch.) After also striking out with Mexico City, Seoul, and Toronto, Dallas finally sold its PCCs to Boston in 1958-59, where they became known to fans as the 'Texas Rangers', soldiering on until 1981 when they were retired from passenger service. Six ended up at Seashore Railway Museum, Kennebunkport, Maine.

While No. 1009 will wear the Dallas Railway & Terminal livery on its return to service, this streetcar has actually been a San Francisco Muni streetcar all its life. It ran from 1948 until 1982 on Muni's J, K, L, M, and N lines, and was then retired and stored. Badly vandalized while in storage, its restoration returns it to like-new condition, painted to honor Big D.

builder
St. Louis Car Co., 1948

modifier
Brookville Equipment Co., 2011

seats
60

weight
40,100 lb. (18,200 kg)

length
50'5" (15.4m)

width
9'0" (2.7m)

height
10'1" (3.1m)

motors
four General Electric 1220E1

control
General Electric

trucks
St. Louis B-3

brakes
Westinghouse electric

Before restoration

Jeremy Whiteman photo

Fully restored

builder
St. Louis Car Co., 1948

modifier
Morrison-Knudsen, 1995

seats
60

weight
40,100 lb. (18,200 kg)

length
50'5" (15.4m)

width
9'0" (2.7m)

height
10'1" (3.1m)

motors
four G.E. 1220E1

control
G.E.

trucks
St. Louis B-3

brakes
Westinghouse electric

Built in 1948 for San Francisco Municipal Railway. Served San Francisco from 1948-present. Painted in tribute to San Francisco Muni (1940s).

This car is painted in tribute to the 'Magic Carpets', as Muni's first five modern-design streetcars were known.

When the PCC streetcar debuted in 1936, some cities lined up quickly to buy them, but in San Francisco, the privately-owned Market Street Railway Co. couldn't afford further capital investments, while the Municipal Railway was prohibited by the City Charter from paying patent royalties covering several PCC features.

Muni's solution was to have these five streetcars custom built without the patented items. The double-end 'Magic Carpets,' numbered from 1001 to 1005, arrived in 1939, wearing this blue & gold livery. They made every other San Francisco streetcar look old-fashioned with their sleek appearance, which even included wheel covers that made the cars look like they were hovering, rather than rolling, along the street—hence the nickname.

While the five cars looked identical, they featured a mix of trucks and controls, perhaps to evaluate options for future purchases. As it turned out, of course, World War II precluded any thought of buying more for the duration.

By the time Muni had funding for more new streetcars, St. Louis Car Company, which built the 'Magic Carpets', had revamped its PCC design, and, importantly, the city had repealed the regulation that precluded patent payments. Thus, its next purchase, in 1948, while also double-ended and similar in appearance, were true PCCs.

By this time, Muni had moved on to a new green and cream livery (modeled on Nos. 1006 and 1008). All ten of the 1948 cars were delivered in the new livery, but when No. 1010 was restored in the early 1990s, it was painted in the handsome blue and gold livery to honor Muni's first modern, magical streetcars.

All five of the original 'Magic Carpets' were retired by 1959, and only one survives. No. 1003 still carries passengers today at the Western Railway Museum at Rio Vista Junction in Solano County (visitor information is at www.wrm.org).

As for No. 1010 itself, it served Muni's J, K, L, M, and N lines from 1948 to 1982, and was then retired and stored before being fully restored for the opening of the F-line in 1995.

Richard Panse photo

On F-line

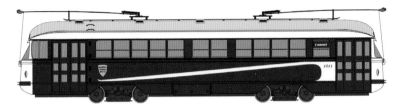

**Built in 1948 for San Francisco Municipal Railway.
Served San Francisco from 1948-present.
Painted in tribute to Market Street Railway Co.**

This streetcar is painted to honor Market Street Railway Co., Muni's private competitor from 1921 to 1944 and the namesake of Muni's current nonprofit preservation partner organization.

While the paint schemes gracing Muni's PCC streetcar fleet almost exclusively represent liveries that actually appeared on similar streetcars in cities around North America, this design is a tribute to what might have been, rather than what actually was. It serves to celebrate the days when streetcars competed side by side for passengers on Market Street, and to make a dream come true.

Market Street Railway Co. drew up plans for a PCC-type double-end streetcar in the late 1930s, hoping to move beyond its old-fashioned boxy streetcars to embrace the streetcar state-of-the-art and compete more effectively against Muni. But the financially troubled Market Street Railway Co. had no way to afford new streetcars and the dream died.

The best they could do was modify the livery on some of their old-fashioned streetcars with a racy white 'zip stripe' slashing across the green side panels along with a bright yellow roof, while retaining the solid white ends patented as a safety feature. That undoubtedly would have been the paint scheme on any PCCs Market Street Railway might have acquired...and now that livery is seen on Market Street 70 years later, on No. 1011.

While it wears the Market Street Railway Co. zip stripe livery today, streetcar No. 1011 has actually been a San Francisco Muni streetcar all its life. It ran from 1948 until 1982 on Muni's J, K, L, M, and N lines, and was then retired and stored. Badly vandalized while in storage, it was fully restored in 2011 by Brookville Equipment Co. in Pennsylvania to operate again as a double-end streetcar...and a dream fulfilled.

builder
St. Louis Car Co., 1948

modifier
Brookville Equipment Co., 2013

seats
60

weight
40,100 lb. (18,200 kg)

length
50'5" (15.4m)

width
9'0" (2.7m)

height
10'1" (3.1m)

motors
four General Electric 1220E1

control
General Electric

trucks
St. Louis B-3

brakes
Westinghouse electric

Roger Goldberg photo

Interior before restoration

Rick Laubscher photo

After restoration

builder
St. Louis Car Co., 1948

modifier
Morrison-Knudsen, 1995

seats
60

weight
40,100 lb. (18,200 kg)

length
50'5" (15.4m)

width
9'0" (2.7m)

height
10'1" (3.1m)

motors
four G.E. 1220E1

control
G.E.

trucks
St. Louis B-3

brakes
Westinghouse electric

**Built in 1948 for San Francisco Municipal Railway.
Served San Francisco from 1948-present.
Painted in tribute to Illinois Terminal Railroad.**

This car is painted to honor Illinois Terminal Railroad System (ITS), which once ran an extensive interurban passenger service in southern Illinois.

Most of its service was run by classic interurban style electric cars. However, buoyed by what turned out to be artificially high ridership during World War II, ITS ordered eight double-end PCC streetcars for its shortest route—a suburban service running six miles from St. Louis, Missouri across the Mississippi River to Granite City, Illinois. Those eight PCCs had bodies identical to No. 1015 (except that the Illinois Terminal cars had no rear doors).

Like their Red Arrow cousins in Philadelphia, the Illinois Terminal PCCs were equipped for multiple unit operation and ran at times in two-car trains. However, despite the modern PCCs, the company saw patronage fall rapidly on the Granite City line as more commuters could afford—and chose—automobiles. The route was abandoned in 1958 and the PCCs were put up for sale. But their lack of rear doors and the high asking price kept buyers at bay.

All but two of the eight Illinois Terminal PCCs were cut up in 1964, but the survivors, Nos. 450 and 451, returned to service in Cleveland from 1975 to 1979, leased from the museums that preserved them to run on the Shaker Heights line during a severe car shortage. But in their brief nine years of service, the big Illinois Terminal PCCs, like their longer-lived Red Arrow cousins, proved their capability in suburban service.

One wonders what might have been if Muni had made the commitment to upgrade the famed interurban 40-line to San Mateo with fast new streetcars like No. 1015, instead of abandoning the line in January 1949. None of Muni's ten new double-end PCCs was even tried on the 40-line in the brief period between the cars' arrival in San Francisco and the line's abandonment, although the long-standing competition from the parallel Southern Pacific commuter trains (now Caltrain) and automobiles had badly undercut ridership, just as for ITS' Granite City line.

Instead, No. 1015 ran on Muni's J, K, L, M, and N lines until 1982, when it was retired and stored for a time until it was restored to serve the new F-line starting in 1995.

David Dugan photo

In demonstration E-line service

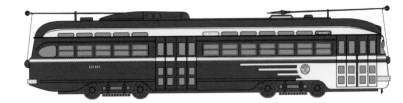

San Francisco, California
Built 1952

**Built in 1952 for San Francisco Municipal Railway.
Served San Francisco from 1952-present.
Painted in its mid-1950s San Francisco Muni livery.**

This is a special streetcar in several ways. No. 1040 is the very last of almost 5,000 'PCC' streetcars manufactured in North America. It was delivered to Muni in 1952, completing an order of 25 PCCs from the venerable St. Louis Car Company. Of all the single-end PCCs in Muni's current active fleet, it is the only one that has worked in San Francisco its entire life.

One goal of the PCC streetcar was to lower costs by requiring only one person to operate it. But San Francisco voters rejected one-operator streetcars, forcing Muni to set up its first modern streetcars with a conductor's station opposite the rear door. After voters changed their minds in 1954, allowing Muni's PCCs to run with a single operator, boarding on No. 1040 and its mates was changed from rear doors to front. At that time, minor changes were made to its as-delivered livery, giving No. 1040 the look it wore for almost a quarter-century and wears again today.

This streetcar was the last to carry riders on Muni's B-Geary line in 1956 (on a charter) but mainly served the J, K, L, M, and N lines, making tens of thousands of trips up and down the surface of Market Street and through city neighborhoods. In the late 1970s, No. 1040 was given a new look, repainted in the white, orange and golden yellow Muni livery created by famed San Francisco designer Walter Landor. The interior was painted white and its seats upholstered in tan vinyl.

When Muni bought modern light rail vehicles and put its streetcar lines in a new subway under Market Street in the early 1980s, it looked like No. 1040 was out of a job. But it went back to work as part of the 'Trolley Festival' summer fleet in 1983, proving the concept of vintage streetcar service that became the permanent F-line. No. 1040 has now been returned to like-new condition, preserving as many original features as possible—including that conductor's seat.

The first streetcar of this class, No. 1016, has been beautifully and faithfully restored by the Western Railway Museum in Solano County. Nine more cars of this class are stored by Muni, four of them repurchased by Market Street Railway and donated back to Muni for possible future restoration.

builder
St. Louis Car Co., 1948

modifier
Brookville Equipment Co., 2011

seats
58

weight
37,600 lb. (17,060 kg)

length
46'5" (14.1m)

width
9'0" (2.7m)

height
10'3" (3.1m)

motors
four Westinghouse 1432K

control
Westinghouse PA

trucks
St. Louis B-3

brakes
Westinghouse electric

Peter Ehrlich photo

No. 1040 in 'Landor' livery, 1984

Adolfo Echeverry photo

Fully restored

builder
St. Louis Car Co., 1948

modifier
Morrison-Knudsen, 1994
Brookville Equipment Co., 2017

seats
47

weight
38,000 lb. (17,200 kg)

length
48'5" (14.8m)

width
8'4" (2.5m)

height
10'3" (3.1m)

motors
four Westinghouse 1432J

trucks
B-2

brakes
electric

Built in 1948 for Philadelphia, Pennsylvania.
Served Philadelphia from 1948-89.
Purchased by Muni in 1992.
Painted in tribute to St. Louis Public Service Co.

The streamlined designed PCC streetcar once ran in 33 cities across North America, but many would say if the PCC had a 'home' it was St. Louis, in large part because of St. Louis Car Company, which built 75% of U.S. PCCs, including every PCC streetcar Muni has ever owned.

Of the thousands of PCCs that rolled off the St. Louis Car Company assembly lines, 300 went to work on the Streets of St. Louis itself. St. Louis Public Service Company (SLPS) was the city's transit operator, acquiring its PCCs in batches of 100 in 1940, 1941, and 1946. After World War II, transit demand dropped in St. Louis as elsewhere, and the number of St. Louis streetcar lines was gradually pared back, with surplus PCCs sold off to such cities as Philadelphia, Shaker Heights, Ohio, and Tampico, Mexico.

But the biggest single batch of St. Louis Public Service PCCs came west to San Francisco in a 1957 lease deal. Those 66 cars, augmented by four more in 1962, allowed Muni to complete conversion of its five streetcar lines, the J, K, L, M, and N to the modern PCCs from their boxy antique predecessors, which had come to be known as 'Iron Monsters.' St. Louis Public Service was taken over by a government agency in 1963, and the last streetcar left the streets of St. Louis in 1966.

Those 70 SLPS PCCs that came to Muni soldiered on until 1982. In fact, one of Muni's ex-SLPS cars, No. 1128, was repainted into its original St. Louis livery and given back its original SLPS number, 1704, to appear in the San Francisco Historic Trolley Festivals through 1987. Muni still retains a number of actual ex-SLPS PCCs, but all need complete rehabilitation to run again. So, in 2016 it was decided to honor St. Louis by repainting Car No. 1050 in SLPS livery. (It had originally been painted in the Muni 'Wings' livery when the F-line opened, but three original Muni cars were subsequently restored in the 'Wings,' making No. 1050 available to represent another city.)

As for St. Louis Car Company, it built its last PCC in 1952. That car, Muni's No. 1040, has been restored to its original appearance—and 'Wings' livery—and still operates as part of the Muni fleet today.

SLPS No. 1704 (later Muni No. 1028) braves the St. Louis snow

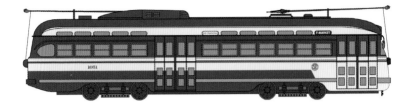

Built in 1948 for Philadelphia, Pennsylvania.
Served Philadelphia from 1948-89.
Purchased by Muni in 1992.
Painted in tribute to San Francisco Muni (1960s).

All of San Francisco's vintage streetcars have interesting histories, but No. 1051 has been adding to its legacy in recent years.

While this was originally a Philadelphia streetcar, it, like No. 1050, was painted in a Muni livery when it joined the San Francisco fleet to open the F-line in 1995. To be specific, it's painted in the 'simplified' green and cream livery that supplanted the famous 'Wings' seen on several streetcars in the historic fleet. The change came after Muni started putting large ads on the sides of its PCCs around 1960 to generate more revenue. These covered up parts of the Wings motif. So, starting in 1963, repainted streetcars sported a simpler cream band running along the side panels of the car. This streetcar is painted in tribute to that scheme.

Many of Muni's PCCs escaped the simplified scheme, running in their (fading) Wings to the end of their original service life in 1982. For a brief time, at the end of the 1970s, there were actually four paint schemes on Muni's PCCs. Eleven streetcars acquired third-hand from Toronto in 1974 had their lower half repainted a dark red and adorned with Muni's short-lived ribbon logo, modeled after the end of the California Street cable cars. The rest of the cars remained in the Toronto livery. And 30 Muni PCCs were repainted in 1978-79 in the new white, orange, and poppy scheme developed by famed designer Walter Landor, along with his new, squiggly Muni logo, immediately dubbed the 'Worm' and still in use today.

But the simplified paint scheme was the most commonly seen on Muni's PCCs in the 1970s. Because of that, No. 1051 was chosen to appear in the film *Milk*, released in 2008. The following year, No. 1051 was dedicated to the memory of the movie's subject, Supervisor Harvey Milk, San Francisco's first openly gay elected official and a champion of public transit, who regularly rode streetcars wearing this paint scheme on the same stretch of Market Street between his home in the Castro and his office in City Hall, where the F-line now runs.

Muni still owns some unrestored PCCs from its original fleet, many of them painted in the simplified scheme. If more streetcars are needed for the active fleet in the future, an original Muni PCC might take over the simplified scheme, allowing the streetcar honoring Harvey Milk to be one he may have actually ridden. If that came to pass, No. 1051, like No. 1050, could be a candidate for another city's PCC livery in the future.

builder
St. Louis Car Co., 1948

modifier
Morrison-Knudsen, 1994
Brookville Equipment Co., 2016

seats
47

weight
38,000 lb. (17,200 kg)

length
48'5" (14.8m)

width
8'4" (2.5m)

height
10'3" (3.1m)

motors
four Westinghouse 1432J

trucks
B-2

brakes
electric

Kevin Sheridan photo

On J-line

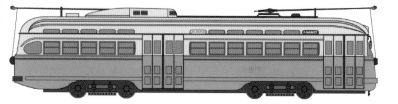

builder
St. Louis Car Co., 1948

modifier
Morrison-Knudsen, 1994

seats
47

weight
38,000 lb. (17,200 kg)

length
48'5" (14.8m)

width
8'4" (2.5m)

height
10'3" (3.1m)

motors
four Westinghouse 1432J

trucks
B-2

brakes
electric

Built in 1948 for Philadelphia, Pennsylvania.
Served Philadelphia from 1948-89.
Purchased by Muni in 1992.
Painted in tribute to Los Angeles Railway Co.

This streetcar is painted to commemorate Los Angeles Railway (LARy). Los Angeles ran PCC streetcars from 1937 to 1963. San Diego got California's first PCCs, beating LARy by a few weeks, but LARy got bragging rights when Shirley Temple, then America's biggest child star, unveiled its first PCCs on March 23, 1937.

The Deco PCCs immediately caught LA's attention, especially when compared to the spindly and odd-looking streetcars that then dominated LARy. The nascent LARy was purchased in 1898 by Henry E. Huntington, nephew of Collis P. Huntington, one of the 'Big Four' magnates who built the mighty Southern Pacific Railroad, long the dominant force in California politics. Huntington built LARy into a strong urban system, with as many as twenty lines and 1,250 streetcars, largely serving central Los Angeles on narrow gauge (3'6", same as San Francisco's cable cars) track.

The average Angeleno knew LARy as the 'Yellow Car' system, for the color of its cars. Its counterpart, Pacific Electric (PE), started by Huntington in 1901 and known as the 'Red Car' system, was more of an interurban operation with a few PCCs on its line from downtown LA to Burbank and Glendale. The two-tone yellow cars had a simple livery compared to the flashy PCC paint scheme. The LARy streetcars never even carried their owner's logo, even though the company had an attractive one.

Henry Huntington died in 1927, ten years before LARy got its first PCCs. But the seeds of the system's future problems had already been planted, as Southern California was starting to become the most automobile-oriented place in the world. LARy did see an incredible spike in ridership during World War II, largely caused by people who already owned automobiles being forced back onto transit by gasoline and tire rationing.

At the peak of patronage, in January 1945, the Huntington estate sold LARy to the consortium of oil, tire, and bus interests managed by National City Lines (NCL). The simple two-tone yellow paint scheme gave way to the standard NCL 'fruit salad' livery modeled by streetcar No. 1080, and an era in Los Angeles streetcar history ended.

Yet, Los Angeles' meticulously maintained narrow gauge PCCs outlasted their standard gauge PE counterparts, and even after leaving LA, many of the LARy cars soldiered on for decades more in their second home—Cairo, Egypt.

On F-line

Built in 1948 for Philadelphia, Pennsylvania.
Served Philadelphia from 1947–92.
Purchased by Muni in 1993.
Painted in tribute to Brooklyn, New York.

This streetcar is painted to honor Brooklyn, which ran PCC streetcars from 1936 to 1956. Trolleys (as they were called there) were once such a part of the Brooklyn scene that the local baseball club was named the 'Trolley Dodgers', later shortened to, well...you know.

The Brooklyn & Queens Transit Corporation (B&QT) was one of the most active participants in the Electric Railway Presidents' Conference Committee (ERPCC) that designed the PCC streetcar. B&QT provided the ERPCC with laboratory space at one of its depots, as well as test trackage and a streetcar to be used for testing trucks and electrical equipment. B&QT was the first to test a PCC prototype, and joined Pittsburgh and Chicago as the first to operate production PCCs in late 1936.

Brooklyn took delivery of 100 PCCs, all but the first one built by St. Louis Car Company. Like many PCC adopters, the transit company chose to draw attention to its new streetcars with a new paint scheme. In B&QT's case, it was an unusual color DuPont called Pachyderm Gray, a warm, brownish shade, accented with a bright scarlet stripe under the windows and a blue-green stripe lower down.

Brooklyn had dozens of streetcar lines crisscrossing the borough and crossing the Brooklyn and Williamsburg Bridges into Manhattan, but the PCCs primarily served only three routes: 67-Seventh Ave.; 68-Smith-Coney Island; and 69-McDonald-Vanderbilt.

In 1940, the New York City Board of Transportation took over B&QT, but no additional PCCs ever joined the Brooklyn fleet. Mayor Fiorello LaGuardia didn't like streetcars, preferring buses instead, but finances and World War II were bigger barriers. But the 100 Brooklyn PCCs soldiered on, their original paint scheme replaced in 1946 by the light green and silver livery modeled on No. 1053. Service across the Brooklyn Bridge to the Park Row terminal in Manhattan, a highlight of any Brooklyn PCC tour, ended in 1950, and by 1956, PCCs were completely gone from Dodgerland...only a year, as it turned out, before the Dodgers left themselves.

builder
St. Louis Car Co., 1948

modifier
Morrison-Knudsen, 1994

seats
47

weight
38,000 lb. (17,200 kg)

length
48'5" (14.8m)

width
8'4" (2.5m)

height
10'3" (3.1m)

motors
four Westinghouse 1432J

trucks
B-2

brakes
electric

Richard Panse photo

On F-line

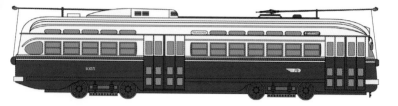

builder
St. Louis Car Co., 1948

modifier
Morrison-Knudsen, 1993
Brookville Equipment Co., 2017

seats
47

weight
38,000 lb. (17,200 kg)

length
48'5" (14.8m)

width
8'4" (2.5m)

height
10'3" (3.1m)

motors
four Westinghouse 1432J

trucks
B-2

brakes
electric

**Built in 1948 for Philadelphia Transportation Co.
Served Philadelphia from 1948-89.
Purchased by Muni in 1992.
Painted in its Philadelphia, Pennsylvania livery.**

The 'City of Brotherly Love' first ran PCC streetcars in 1938 (Muni No. 1060 wears the original silver paint scheme).

After World War II, Philadelphia Transportation Co. (PTC) ordered 210 more PCCs from St. Louis Car Company. This car, numbered 2122 in Philly (now Muni No. 1055), was delivered in 1948 wearing this livery of green, cream, and red. The city later added 90 secondhand PCCs from Kansas City and St. Louis in the 1950s.

But National City Lines, owned by bus, tire, and gasoline companies, gained control of PTC and began gradually converting the system to buses. Between 1954 and 1958, almost 1,000 Philadelphia streetcars were scrapped as three quarters of the city's streetcar lines were either converted to buses or discontinued altogether. In the process, many surviving PCCs were reassigned to new lines. This car was shifted in 1955 to the 15-Girard line.

But with PTC spending as little as possible on streetcar maintenance, service steadily deteriorated, a decline that continued after the Southeastern Pennsylvania Transportation Authority (SEPTA, a public agency) took over the transit system in 1968. Several lines, including the 15-Girard, "temporarily" converted to buses, conversions that lasted for years or forever, because of a lack of operable streetcars.

In the early 1980s, SEPTA replaced PCCs on its subway-surface routes with new light rail vehicles built by Kawasaki of Japan. By the early 1990s, all of Philadelphia's PCCs had been retired from service.

Muni bought and rebuilt 14 of SEPTA's PCCs to inaugurate F-line service in 1995, at a time when no PCCs were left running in Philadelphia. But inspired in part by the F-line, some Philadelphians demanded restoration of PCC service in their own town, and got it in 2005 on the 15-Girard line (albeit with heavily modified streetcars using a different propulsion system). The Girard cars are painted in a version of No. 1055's historic livery.

Jeremy Whiteman photo

At Castro Street F-line terminal

Built in 1948 for Philadelphia Transportation Co.
Served Philadelphia from 1948-89.
Purchased by Muni in 1992.
Painted in tribute to Kansas City, Missouri/Kansas.

This car is painted in tribute to Kansas City, which ran PCC streetcars from 1941 to 1957. Kansas City's PCCs—184 in all—were painted to emphasize their modern lines, with a black 'swoosh' on the sides to highlight the logo of Kansas City Public Service Company (KCPS), which featured Frederic Remington's famed sculpture "The Scout" overlaid on a red heart.

KCPS initially planned for a PCC fleet of 371 cars, but only 24 had been delivered by America's entry into World War II. As in other cities, war production priorities deferred dreams of all-PCC service in Kansas City. After the war, KCPS took delivery of 160 more PCCs, though they almost cancelled some of those because of shaky finances.

Kansas City is actually two municipalities split by the Missouri-Kansas border. KCPS streetcars served both, but rapidly lost ridership as people moved to the suburbs, beyond the ends of the lines. Kansas City's 25 streetcar lines dwindled to three, which finally ceased service in 1957. One of the three was the famous 56-Country Club—known as the 'Club Line'—which wound south from downtown on an old steam railroad right-of-way, sharing its tracks with electric freight trains.

Many of Kansas City's PCCs were scrapped after unsuccessful attempts to find buyers. (Muni was approached to buy KCPS' last 41 PCCs in 1957, but declined, lacking the funding.) But some Kansas City PCCs were sold to other cities, including Toronto. Eleven of these ended up at Muni after all, coming third-hand in 1970 to help carry streetcar passengers on the J, K, L, M, and N lines on detours that were required to build the Market Street subway. These ex-Kansas City PCCs ran in San Francisco between 1973 and 1979, as Nos. 1180 to 1190, before being retired. Most were subsequently scrapped.

One ex-Kansas City and was put on display for a time at Union Station, which is now the terminal of the modern streetcar line that opened in Kansas City in 2016.

builder
St. Louis Car Co., 1948

modifier
Morrison-Knudsen, 1993
Brookville Equipment Co., 2016

seats
47

weight
38,000 lb. (17,200 kg)

length
48'5" (14.8m)

width
8'4" (2.5m)

height
10'3" (3.1m)

motors
four Westinghouse 1432J

trucks
B-2

brakes
electric

Kevin Sheridan photo

On The Embarcadero

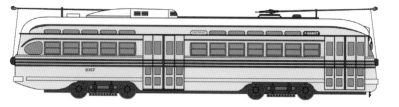

1057

builder
St. Louis Car Co., 1948

modifier
Morrison-Knudsen, 1993

seats
47

weight
38,000 lb. (17,200 kg)

length
48′5″ (14.8m)

width
8′4″ (2.5m)

height
10′3″ (3.1m)

motors
four Westinghouse 1432J

trucks
B-2

brakes
electric

**Built in 1948 for Philadelphia Transportation Co.
Served Philadelphia from 1948-89.
Purchased by Muni in 1992.
Painted in tribute to Cincinnati, Ohio.**

This streetcar is painted to honor Cincinnati, which ran PCC streetcars from 1939 to 1951. Cincinnati was unique among North American streetcar systems in requiring two overhead wires for streetcars, one to supply electrical power, the other to provide a ground to complete the circuit. This arrangement grew from an early and (pardon the pun) groundless fear of electrocution from the standard streetcar practice of returning current through the tracks. (Trolley buses use two wires because they run on rubber tires and have no tracks to use as ground.)

The uniqueness of Cincinnati's PCCs extended to the paint scheme, an eye-popping canary yellow with three bold green stripes around the body. Only PCCs got this treatment in Cincinnati—buses and older streetcars were painted a prosaic transit orange.

Cincinnati's streetcar governance was also unusual. The system was owned by a private company, the Cincinnati Street Railway Co. (CSR), but the City of Cincinnati had direct control over routes and operations.

In 1939, CSR purchased three modern streetcars—competing PCCs from St. Louis Car Co. and Pullman-Standard, plus a Brilliner—to compare their features. It then bought 26 PCCs from St. Louis Car Co. in 1940 and 25 more that were delivered in 1947. CSR wanted 50 PCCs in that post-war order, but the City government, which favored buses, cut the order in half. Then, with the paint on the new PCCs still shiny, the city forced conversion of the Madisonville line to trolley buses in July 1947—one of the earliest abandonments of a PCC route in America—and followed with demands for more conversions.

By 1950, with its finances in disarray, CSR decided to sell its PCCs, half of which were just three years old. Toronto bought all but the Pullman-Standard demonstrator, which, along with the single Brilliner, joined older Peter Witt style streetcars in running out the clock. It was the only time that PCCs were outlasted in regular service by old-fashioned streetcars.

Cincinnati's last streetcar line, the 78-Lockland, was abandoned on April 29, 1951. Sixty-five years later, Cincinnati opened a modern streetcar line connecting downtown and the Reds' ballpark with the historic Over-the-Rhine neighborhood.

Its vivid color makes No. 1057 one of the most photographed streetcars on the F-line.

Rick Laubscher photo

On the Embarcadero

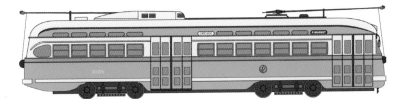

Built in 1948 for Philadelphia Transportation Co.
Served Philadelphia from 1948-89.
Purchased by Muni in 1992.
Painted in tribute to Chicago, Illinois.

This streetcar is painted to honor Chicago, which ran PCC streetcars from 1936 to 1958. Chicago had the largest PCC fleet ever purchased new by one city—683 cars. Chicago's first PCCs hit the streets in November 1936. At 50'5" they were the longest single-end PCCs ever built, and boasted three sets of doors to swallow crowds quickly. Each PCC carried two crew members. Passengers boarded through three pairs of double doors at the rear of the car, paid their fare, and moved forward, exiting through doors either at the center or front of the car. The design worked well and Chicago stuck to it, though no other city followed suit.

The first Chicago PCCs were nicknamed 'Blue Geese' after their paint scheme, so it was natural that the cars delivered in green after the war would be dubbed 'Green Hornets' after the then-popular radio serial.

Chicago Transit Authority closed its last streetcar line in 1958, but its PCC streetcar fleet "died and went to heaven," because many parts of the cars were used in new PCC elevated trains used on the famous Loop.

PCC days in the Windy City were immortalized in the song 'Old Days', by the rock group Chicago (the group was originally named Chicago Transit Authority):

> Old days, good times I remember
> gold days, days I'll always treasure
> funny faces, full of love and laughter
> funny places, summer nights and streetcars
> take me back to a world gone away
> boyhood memories, seem like yesterday

When the F-line opened in 1995, car No. 1058 was painted in the final 1950s Chicago Transit Authority PCC livery of green and cream. However, when it was repainted in 2010, it was switched to the more famous Green Hornet livery of 'Mercury Green, Croydon Cream, and Swampholly Orange', adopted in the era immediately following World War II.

No. 1058 is a fitting tribute to the place Carl Sandburg called "The City of Big Shoulders"—and Big PCCs!

builder
St. Louis Car Co., 1948

modifier
Morrison-Knudsen, 1993

seats
47

weight
38,000 lb. (17,200 kg)

length
48'5" (14.8m)

width
8'4" (2.5m)

height
10'3" (3.1m)

motors
four Westinghouse 1432J

trucks
B-2

brakes
electric

Rick Laubscher photo

Late 1950s CTA livery worn by No. 1058 when the F-line opened

Jeremy Whiteman photo

Classic 'Green Hornet' livery now on No. 1058

BOSTON ELEVATED RAILWAY

builder
St. Louis Car Co., 1948

modifier
Morrison-Knudsen, 1993
Brookville Equipment Co., 2017

seats
47

weight
38,000 lb. (17,200 kg)

length
48'5" (14.8m)

width
8'4" (2.5m)

height
10'3" (3.1m)

motors
four Westinghouse 1432J

trucks
B-2

brakes
electric

Kevin Sheridan photo

At Fisherman's Wharf terminal

Built in 1948 for Philadelphia Transportation Co.
Served Philadelphia from 1948-89.
Purchased by Muni in 1992.
Painted in tribute to Boston, Massachusetts.

No U.S. city has had longer or more varied experience with PCC streetcars than Boston. From the delivery of its first streamliner in 1937 until the present day, PCCs have been a part of the Beantown scene. That first PCC was ordered by private operator Boston Elevated Railway Company (BERy) and was followed by twenty more in 1941. No. 1059 is painted in tribute to the BERy era of PCC operation in Boston.

Boston did better than most other cities seeking to expand its PCC fleet during World War II, gaining U.S. government approval for 225 new cars built with controls that allowed two or more cars to be coupled together into trains. Boston's single-end PCCs were unique in the U.S. for having additional doors on the left-hand side to accommodate passengers in Boston's vintage subway.

In 1947, the Commonwealth of Massachusetts bought BERy and operated its lines as part of the Metropolitan Transit Authority (MTA). The MTA upgraded the PCCs it inherited and took delivery of 50 new PCCs in 1951 with large 'picture windows' on the sides. (Though San Francisco ordered its last new PCCs after Boston, Muni chose the traditional design seen on Car No. 1040 instead.)

In 1959, Boston added 25 double-end PCCs recently retired in Dallas, bringing its PCC fleet to an all-time high of 344 cars. The picture window PCCs were assigned to the then-new showcase Riverside line.

In 1964, the MTA became the MBTA (Massachusetts Bay Transportation Authority). The MBTA soon color-coded its rail lines and PCCs (green for most streetcar lines, red for the isolated Mattapan-Ashmont line, which was essentially an extension of the Red Line subway). Mattapan-Ashmont is the only Boston line operated by PCCs today, albeit rebuilt ones that have reverted to an orange and silver variation of the original livery.

In 1973, prodded by the U.S. government, Boston and San Francisco jointly ordered new Boeing light rail vehicles to replace their PCC fleets. The Boeings proved unreliable in both cities, while the reliable PCCs continue to hold the hearts of San Franciscans and Bostonians alike.

Early in the morning of September 2, 1995, No. 1059 was the first car in regular service on the permanent F-line.

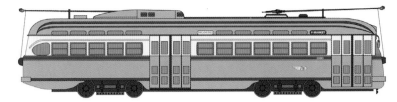

**Built in 1948 for Philadelphia Transportation Co.
Served Philadelphia from 1947-89.
Purchased by Muni in 1992.
Painted in tribute to Philadelphia, Pennsylvania.**

This streetcar is an actual Philadelphia streetcar painted in that city's original PCC livery, dating from 1938. Although Philadelphia Rapid Transit Co. (PRT) was the largest streetcar operator that was not a member of the coalition that designed the famous PCC streetcar, it was still an early buyer.

Philadelphia's first batch of twenty PCCs ran on Wayne Avenue's Route 53. In 1940, successor company Philadelphia Transportation Co. (PTC) ordered 130 more PCCs, and the following year—worried that impending war would shut off availability of new cars—bought an additional 110. Philly's new PCCs soldiered hard, carrying the wartime crush of riders, and may have saved the system from early bus conversion.

Following World War II, PTC ordered more PCCs. This car was part of that group, arriving new in Philadelphia in 1947, numbered 2715. The later years of the Philadelphia PCC story are recounted in the description of Muni Car No. 1055, which was also part of that postwar Philadelphia PCC purchase.

Car No. 1060, which Muni acquired from Philadelphia in 1992 as part of the initial F-line fleet, models the original PTC livery of silver with cream window area and electric blue striping. The similarity to the packaging of Kraft's famous 'Philadelphia Cream Cheese' did not go unnoticed, providing the car a nickname—the Cream Cheese Car.

When it originally went into Muni service in 1995, car No. 1060 was painted to represent Newark, New Jersey. In November 2002, the car suffered severe body damage when she took a curve at Market and Steuart too fast, jumped the track, and hit a lightpost. After extensive repairs, Muni repainted No. 1060 in this 1938 silver and blue Philadelphia livery to replace the paint scheme in Muni's fleet previously worn by wrecked PCC No. 1054. In turn, the Newark livery that had been on No. 1060 was applied by Muni to a streetcar that actually ran in Newark, No. 1070.

builder
St. Louis Car Co., 1947

modifier
Morrison-Knudsen, 1993
Brookville Equipment Co., 2016

seats
47

weight
38,000 lb. (17,200 kg)

length
48'5" (14.8m)

width
8'4" (2.5m)

height
10'3" (3.1m)

motors
four Westinghouse 1432J

trucks
B-2

brakes
electric

Jeremy Whiteman photo

On F-line at Fisherman's Wharf

builder
St. Louis Car Co., 1948

modifier
Morrison-Knudsen, 1993

seats
47

weight
38,000 lb. (17,200 kg)

length
48'5" (14.8m)

width
8'4" (2.5m)

height
10'3" (3.1m)

motors
four Westinghouse 1432J

trucks
B-2

brakes
electric

Richard Panse photo

On The Embarcadero

**Built in 1948 for Philadelphia Transportation Co.
Served Philadelphia from 1948-89.
Purchased by Muni in 1992.
Painted in tribute to Pacific Electric, So. California.**

Southern California once boasted one of the great interurban systems in the world—the mighty Pacific Electric (PE)—running from LA east to San Bernardino, west to Santa Monica, south to Long Beach and beyond as far as Newport Beach. The 'Big Red Cars', as all PE equipment was known to Southern Californians, covered hundreds of miles of track. Developed by Henry Huntington, nephew of one of the titans who built the Southern Pacific Railroad, the PE contributed significantly to the development of Southern California, by Huntington's design. Neighborhoods and even whole cities, including the modestly named Huntington Beach, came into existence as a direct result of PE service.

Huntington owned a second streetcar system, Los Angeles Railway (represented in Muni's fleet by Car No. 1052), which served the more urbanized core of LA and actually carried more passengers than PE.

In 1940, PE bought 30 PCCs in a unique design, double-ended with front and center doors. The decision may have been partly politically driven. In 1936, PE had largely converted its line connecting Downtown LA with Glendale and Burbank to buses. Residents complained so loudly to the California State Railroad Commission that PE was pressured to restore full-time rail service and used the PCCs to do so.

Trains of up to three PCCs ran from the Subway Terminal Building downtown through a tunnel almost a mile long, and then over trestles, streets, and private rights-of-way to Burbank and Glendale. For a time in the early 1940s, PCCs helped out on the busy Venice-Hollywood line as well.

Three years after their 1955 retirement, the thirty PE PCCs were sold to Buenos Aires, Argentina, where they served only briefly. Then, in 1960, the Los Angeles Metropolitan Transit Authority (LAMTA), successor to both PE and LA Railway, fitted out a single-end ex-LA Railway PCC with standard gauge trucks (borrowed from Muni!) and tested it on PE's former (but still busy) LA-Long Beach line. Maybe the test would have worked better if they had used larger, multiple-unit, double-end PCCs, like the ones they had just shipped to South America!

Muni No. 1061 is painted in the red, orange, and silver livery of the PE PCCs, inspired by the 'Daylight' train colors of PE's big brother Southern Pacific. Today, every F-line trip passes SP's old headquarters at One Market Street.

Built in 1948 for Philadelphia Transportation Co.
Served Philadelphia from 1948-89.
Purchased by Muni in 1992.
Painted in tribute to Pittsburgh Railways Co.

The 'Steel City,' as Pittsburgh has long been called, was also one of the great PCC streetcar cities as well. It operated the world's first PCC carrying paying passengers, in 1936. Its 666 PCCs were second in number to Chicago's 683 among U.S. operators. It operated PCCs until 1999, one of the longest tenures of any PCC operator.

Pittsburgh Railways Company began the PCC era with Car No. 100, which went into service shortly before Brooklyn's first PCCs did. Pittsburgh rapidly expanded its PCC fleet in a bid to modernize its extensive streetcar system, which once numbered 68 lines. A hilly city like San Francisco, Pittsburgh's PCCs routinely climbed grades far steeper than Muni's PCCs had to handle.

Pittsburgh's PCCs ran through prestigious neighborhoods, working-class enclaves, past downtown high-rises and factory areas. They even ran along two interurban lines way out into the country, 29 and 36 miles long. (The longer line would be equivalent to a Muni PCC running from the Ferry Building to Palo Alto!)

Streetcar service in Pittsburgh waned rapidly after 1959, and Pittsburgh Railways sold the remaining operation to the Port Authority of Allegheny County in 1964. Like Muni, Pittsburgh opened a downtown rail subway in the 1980s and bought new light rail vehicles to serve the subway and replace the PCCs. A handful of PCCs were rebuilt in-house and served an outlying line until 1999. Muni purchased two of those home-built Pittsburgh PCCs in the early 2000s, but has elected to date not to restore them, given their non-standard features.

So Car No. 1062 now honors Pittsburgh's extensive PCC operation, after spending its first 21 years in Muni service painted in tribute to Louisville, Kentucky, a city that bought, but never operated, PCCs after World War II.

builder
St. Louis Car Co., 1948

modifier
Morrison-Knudsen, 1993
Brookville Equipment Co., 2017

seats
47

weight
38,000 lb. (17,200 kg)

length
48'5" (14.8m)

width
8'4" (2.5m)

height
10'3" (3.1m)

motors
four Westinghouse 1432J

trucks
B-2

brakes
electric

A PCC in Pittsburgh

David Dugan photo

No. 1062 when painted
in tribute to Louisville

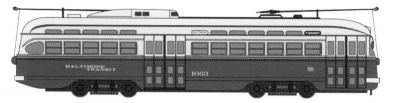

builder
St. Louis Car Co., 1948

modifier
Morrison-Knudsen, 1993
Brookville Equipment Co., 2017

seats
47

weight
38,000 lb. (17,200 kg)

length
48'5" (14.8m)

width
8'4" (2.5m)

height
10'3" (3.1m)

motors
four Westinghouse 1432J

trucks
B-2

brakes
electric

S. Thurmovik photo

Car No. 7407 at Baltimore
Streetcar Museum

Jeremy Whiteman photo

Car No. 1063 in earlier yellow livery

**Built in 1948 for Philadelphia Transportation Co.
Served Philadelphia from 1948-89.
Purchased by Muni in 1992.
Painted in tribute to Baltimore, Maryland.**

This car is painted to honor Baltimore, which ran
PCC streetcars from 1936 to 1963. One of the first
cities to operate PCCs, Baltimore began with an
order of 27 in 1936. The privately owned operator,
Baltimore Transit Company (BTC), subsequently
placed seven additional orders for the streamliners,
eventually acquiring 275 PCCs. They made up just
over a quarter of BTC's huge streetcar fleet, which
also included a variety of old-fashioned cars and
150 lightweight high-speed Peter Witt cars ordered
in 1930.

The Baltimore system included some spectacular
trackage, including lots of private rights-of-way,
viaducts, and a drawbridge. PCCs served all of
it, in part because BTC would mix PCCs in with
older streetcars on every line. Most companies
tried to operate complete lines with PCCs to take
advantage of the streamliners' quicker acceleration.
In Baltimore, motormen had to rein in their PCC
'steeds' lest they catch up to the 'old plug' wooden
streetcars filling the run ahead of them.

National City Lines bought up BTC stock during
World War II, assuming operational control in late
1945. Soon after, many of BTC's 29 streetcar lines
started converting to buses (made by NCL owner
General Motors). While it is true that sixteen of
those lines used antique wooden streetcars and
had worn out tracks and car barns, it is also true
that BTC cancelled an order for 100 multiple-unit
PCCs in 1946. It is true as well that flight from the
inner city to suburbs proceeded faster in postwar
Baltimore than in most other U.S. cities.

These factors combined to doom Baltimore's
streetcar system. After steady attrition, the end
came on November 3, 1963, when car No. 7407
(now at the Baltimore Streetcar Museum) limped
into the barn to close out Baltimore's PCC era.
Car No. 1063 is now painted in the original Baltimore
Transit livery of blue, cream, orange, and gray. From
1995 to 2016, it was painted in the later yellow
Baltimore livery.

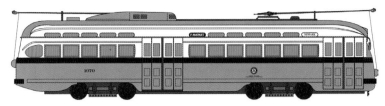

Built in 1946 for Twin City Rapid Transit Co.,
Minneapolis-St. Paul, Minnesota.
Served Minneapolis-St. Paul from 1946-53.
Served Newark, New Jersey from 1953-2001.
Purchased by Muni in 2004.
Painted in its orginal Newark, New Jersey livery.

Across New York Harbor from Manhattan, streetcars
survived long after Gotham gave them up. In
Newark, New Jersey, an old canal bed became a
streetcar right-of-way, with part covered over to
form what was called the City Subway.

In 1953, Newark's old streetcars were replaced
by thirty PCC streetcars puchased secondhand
from Twin City Rapid Transit of Minneapolis-St.
Paul, Minnesota. These cars were just five to seven
years old at the time they came to Newark, serving
the transit agency then called Public Service
Coordinated Transport. Separated from street
traffic, stored under cover and well maintained,
these cars provided reliable service for a half-
century until New Jersey Transit, the state operating
agency that had taken over the Newark City
Subway, replaced the PCCs with light rail vehicles
(LRVs) in 2001.

Muni purchased eleven of the ex-Twin Cities, ex-
Newark cars in 2004 and renovated them to meet
growing rider demands on Market Street and The
Embarcadero.

This car's exterior is painted in the 1950s livery
it first wore in Newark, including the unique red
wheels, source of its 'Ruby Slippers' nickname. Toto,
we're not in New Jersey anymore!

PUBLIC SERVICE
COORDINATED TRANSPORT

builder
St. Louis Car Co., 1946

modifier
Brookville Equipment Co., 2004

seats
50

weight
37,600 lb. (17,060 kg)

length
46'5" (14.1m)

width
9'0" (2.7m)

height
10'3" (3.1m)

motors
four General Electric 1220

trucks
B-2

brakes
electric

Jeremy Whiteman photo

At Muni's Cameron Beach Yard

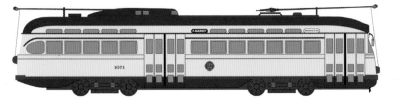

builder
St. Louis Car Co., 1947

modifier
Morrison-Knudsen, 1993

seats
47

weight
38,000 lb. (17,200 kg)

length
48'5" (14.8m)

width
8'4" (2.5m)

height
10'3" (3.1m)

motors
four Westinghouse 1432J

trucks
B-2

brakes
electric

Built in 1947 for Twin City Rapid Transit Co., Minneapolis-St. Paul, Minnesota.
Served Minneapolis-St. Paul from 1947-53.
Served Newark, New Jersey from 1953-2001.
Purchased by Muni in 2004.
Painted in its original Minneapolis-St. Paul livery.

Minneapolis-St. Paul came late to PCC streetcars. Its private operator, Twin City Rapid Transit, was fiercely proud of its own car-building capabilities, and even sold cars it built to other properties. So, they had no interest in participating in the industry group that designed the PCC in the mid-1930s.

As World War II took a toll on TCRT's all-wooden streetcar fleet, though, management gave in, first acquiring a demonstrator PCC in 1945, then placing three successive orders from St. Louis Car Company. The bodies were built extra tough for the demanding Minnesota winters.

The first group of forty cars required a crew of two people, motorman and conductor, like Muni's first PCCs. When that requirement was eased, though, the conductor's station was removed and later orders were designed for single-person operation.

The PCC era in Minneapolis-St. Paul ended up being one of the shortest anywhere. A battle for control of Twin City Rapid Transit ended with all streetcar lines being converted to buses by June 1954. Its PCCs, still almost like new, all found new homes quickly. Of the 141 Twin City PCCs, 91 went to Mexico City, twenty went to Shaker Heights, Ohio, and thirty went to Newark, New Jersey, where they served another half-century on the 'City Subway' line.

Eleven of these Twin Cities-turned-Newark cars were purchased by Muni in 2004 and renovated for F-line service, including this one, TCRT No. 362. Now Muni No. 1071, it again proudly wears its original Twin City Rapid Transit livery, a striking blend of bright yellow and forest green.

One original Twin City PCC, No. 322, returned to its home city and is now in museum operation on a portion of the historic and scenic Como-Harriet line.

Jeremy Whiteman photo

Passing the Ferry Building

Mexico City, Mexico · Tribute Livery
Built 1946

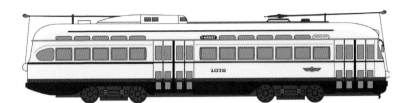

No. 1072

Built in 1946 for Twin City Rapid Transit Co.,
Minneapolis-St. Paul, Minnesota.
Served Minneapolis-St. Paul from 1946-53.
Served Newark, New Jersey from 1953-2001.
Purchased by Muni in 2004.
Painted in tribute to Mexico City, Mexico.

This car is painted to honor Mexico City, which ran
PCC streetcars from 1947 until 1984.

Shortly after taking over a privately owned
tramway company in 1945, the Mexican government
agency Servicio de Transportes Electricos del Distrito
Federal (STE) began a fleet rehabilitation program
that included the order of Mexico's first PCC from
St. Louis Car Co.—the only PCC ever bought new in
Latin America.

Numbered 2000 and dubbed 'La Bella Rosa', it
was placed into premium fare service on the route
to the famed floating gardens at Xochimilco in
1947. No more PCCs joined the Mexico City fleet
until 1954, when 91 PCCs, identical to No. 1072,
arrived secondhand from Twin City Rapid Transit in
Minneapolis-St. Paul. The following year, 183 more
used PCCs arrived from Detroit.

Left-side doors were installed on all these cars to
serve platforms on several routes. By 1957, the entire
Mexico City streetcar system was PCC-operated,
but tracks and cars gradually deteriorated, while
new subway lines offered faster service.

STE tried to spice up the PCC fleet in different
ways, installing new bodies on a few cars and
exchanging the handsome but restrained cream
livery for a flashy red-orange on many cars.

In the 1980s, Mexico City's last PCCs were
replaced by home-built trams, which themselves
used some PCC parts. Mexico's port city of Tampico
also ran PCCs from 1958 to 1974.

Today, San Francisco has many reminders of
its own Mexican past—and present, with a vibrant
Mexican-American community playing a central role
in the community. And now it has another tribute to
Mexico—PCC No. 1072.

builder
St. Louis Car Co., 1946

modifier
Brookville Equipment Co., 2004

seats
50

weight
37,600 lb. (17,060 kg)

length
46'5" (14.1m)

width
9'0" (2.7m)

height
10'3" (3.1m)

motors
four General Electric 1220

trucks
B-2

brakes
electric

Jeremy Whiteman photo

On The Embarcadero

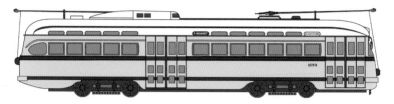

builder
St. Louis Car Co., 1947

modifier
Brookville Equipment Co., 2004

seats
50

weight
37,600 lb. (17,060 kg)

length
46′5″ (14.1m)

width
9′0″ (2.7m)

height
10′3″ (3.1m)

motors
four General Electric 1220

trucks
B-2

brakes
electric

Built in 1947 for Twin City Rapid Transit Co., Minneapolis-St. Paul, Minnesota.
Served Minneapolis-St. Paul from 1947-53.
Served Newark, New Jersey from 1953-2001.
Purchased by Muni in 2004.
Painted in tribute to El Paso, TX/Juarez, Mexico.

This car is painted to honor El Paso, Texas and Juarez, Mexico, which ran PCC streetcars from 1950 to 1973, the only PCC streetcar line to ever cross an international border.

El Paso's PCC streetcars came secondhand from San Diego (see our No. 1078). A bit ironically, the buyer, El Paso City Lines, was owned by National City Lines (NCL), notorious for buying transit systems around the U.S., ripping out the streetcars, and replacing them with buses.

In El Paso, NCL did convert several streetcar lines, but not the international route across the Rio Grande River Bridge into Juarez. First, the line was very profitable. Second, El Paso City Lines only had authority to run streetcars in Mexico—not buses. So they replaced older streetcars with seventeen of the San Diego PCCs in 1947. Because of increased ridership (a rarity for streetcars in that era), they bought three more PCCs in 1952.

Since these PCCs were single-ended, with no turning loop at the carbarn, the cars had to back up a full mile to enter service every day. The traditional front-facing PCC seating (seen on No. 1073) was replaced with continuous longitudinal seating along the walls of the cars so that customs officials could check passengers more quickly as they crossed the Rio Grande.

The international line came to an end in 1973, when Juarez merchants pressured their government to end the concession, believing too many residents were crossing the Rio Grande on the streetcars to shop in El Paso. But ten of the streetcars survive today, with the City of El Paso, now their owner, periodically raising the possibility of restoring some kind of streetcar service there.

National City Lines generally painted the streetcars of its properties in a standard orange, green, and white livery colloquially known as 'fruit salad' and so it was in El Paso initially. The fruit salad paint scheme of National City Lines is modeled (in its Los Angeles version) on Muni No. 1080. But most El Paso streetcars later received different schemes, including this late 1960s version in light green with white and red trim, modeled on No. 1073. The crossed American and Mexican flags on the front provide a nice detail.

Adolfo Echeverry photo

On F-line

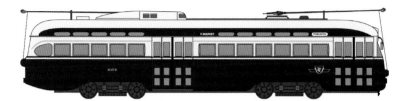

Toronto, Canada · Tribute Livery
Built 1946

Built in 1946 for Twin City Rapid Transit Co.,
Minneapolis-St. Paul, Minnesota.
Served Minneapolis-St. Paul from 1946-53.
Served Newark, New Jersey from 1953-2001.
Purchased by Muni in 2004.
Painted in tribute to Toronto, Ontario, Canada.

This car is painted to honor Toronto, which ran PCC streetcars in regular service from 1938 until 1995. Toronto boasted the largest fleet of PCCs in North America: 745 cars.

Nowhere on the continent have streetcars had such continuing success, with routes running all over Canada's largest city to this day. When the Toronto Transit Commission (TTC) ordered its first PCCs in 1938, the city was already well served by a large fleet of all-steel Peter Witt style streetcars (some of which remained in active service until 1963), but needed more streetcars to meet growing demand. St. Louis Car Company shipped PCC body shells and trucks north for assembly by Canadian Car and Foundry. This became standard practice for Toronto's ongoing purchases of new PCCs.

But the Canadian city was also a prolific buyer of used PCCs, picking up cars after World War II from Cincinnati, Cleveland (including the PCCs originally built for Louisville), Birmingham, and Kansas City. The opening of heavy-rail subways decreased the PCC fleet in the late 1960s, and Toronto began replacing its beloved 'Red Rockets' in the late 1970s with Canadian Light Rail Vehicles (CRLVs), which themselves are in the process of being replaced by yet another generation of Canadian streetcar.

Muni's Historic Trolley Festivals in the 1980s partly inspired the renovation of nineteen PCCs for the new Harbourfront line that opened in 1990, but these were replaced by CLRVs just five years later, leaving only two PCCs in Toronto for charter service (along with one Peter Witt).

In the 1970s Muni acquired eleven ex-Toronto PCCs (originally from Kansas City) for brief service in San Francisco. They essentially kept this same maroon and cream paint scheme, with Muni's 'cable car ribbon' logo replacing the 'TTC' logo. Now, this handsome Red Rocket livery is back on San Francisco's streets to stay.

builder
St. Louis Car Co., 1946

modifier
Brookville Equipment Co., 2004

seats
50

weight
37,600 lb. (17,060 kg)

length
46'5" (14.1m)

width
9'0" (2.7m)

height
10'3" (3.1m)

motors
four General Electric 1220

trucks
B-2

brakes
electric

Jeremy Whiteman photo

On The Embarcadero

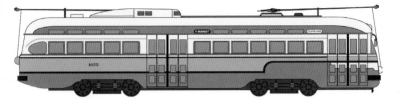

1075

Built in 1946 for Twin City Rapid Transit Co., Minneapolis-St. Paul, Minnesota.
Served Minneapolis-St. Paul from 1946-53.
Served Newark, New Jersey from 1953-2001.
Purchased by Muni in 2004.
Painted in tribute to Cleveland, Ohio.

This car is painted to honor Cleveland Transit System (CTS), which ran PCC streetcars from 1946 to 1953.

Cleveland gained global streetcar fame early in the 20th century when its transit commissioner, Peter Witt, designed a popular pre-PCC streetcar that was adopted by many cities (including Milan, Italy, ten of whose 'Peter Witts' are now part of Muni's historic fleet).

But after World War II, CTS wanted more modern cars, procuring 75 PCCs, including 25 built for Louisville that never ran there (see paint design shown on Muni No. 1062). The Cleveland paint scheme, reminiscent of the Browns football team that debuted the same year as the PCCs, was one of the more intricate to appear on a streetcar.

At the same time, though, CTS was issuing a series of transit master plans that evolved from a system that called for 450 PCCs to one that called for none at all—instead, a rapid transit line fed by trolley buses and motor coaches. By May 1953, CTS had sold and delivered all 75 of its PCCs to Toronto, leaving its remaining streetcar lines to be served by the old Peter Witts until they shut down the following year.

But that wasn't the end of the PCC story in Cleveland. The local government of a suburb, Shaker Heights, had bought out a private transit operator during World War II. By 1948, they began operating PCCs on what was called the 'Shaker Rapid' to downtown Cleveland, mostly along private rights-of-way. Most of the Shaker Heights PCCs, both new and secondhand, were fitted with multiple unit controls and ran in trains of up to four cars. (Some of the Shaker Heights PCCs came from the same original Minneapolis-St. Paul group of cars that include Muni Nos. 1070-1080.)

The Shaker Heights PCCs were replaced in 1983 with light rail vehicles made by Breda of Italy, which also built Muni's current light rail vehicle fleet used on the J, K, L, M, N, and T lines.

builder
St. Louis Car Co., 1946

modifier
Brookville Equipment Co., 2004

seats
50

weight
37,600 lb. (17,060 kg)

length
46'5" (14.1m)

width
9'0" (2.7m)

height
10'3" (3.1m)

motors
four General Electric 1220

trucks
B-2

brakes
electric

Jeremy Whiteman photo

On F-line

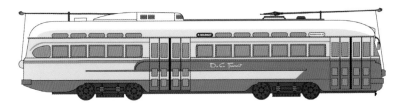

Built in 1946 for Twin City Rapid Transit Co.,
Minneapolis-St. Paul, Minnesota.
Served Minneapolis-St. Paul from 1946-53.
Served Newark, New Jersey from 1953-2001.
Purchased by Muni in 2004.
Painted in tribute to Washington, D.C.

This car's exterior commemorates Washington D.C.,
which operated PCC streetcars from 1937 to 1962.

One early complaint about streetcars was the
visual impact of overhead wires. In 1893, Congress
banned such wires in downtown Washington D.C.,
about the time San Francisco did the same on
Market Street. But in Washington the ban stuck,
requiring a different technology to power streetcars.
Washington put the wire in a conduit between
the rails, making their tracks look just like cable
car tracks. Traditional trolley poles were still used
beyond the protected zone in central Washington.
To transition, a worker stood in a 'plow pit' where
the overhead wires ended and hooked up each
passing streetcar with a 'plow' underneath the car
to connect to the wire in the conduit.

When Washington purchased its 489 streamlined
PCCs beginning in 1937, they had this dual-power
technology. The federal government, which
regulated the private operator, Capital Transit,
provided an incentive by ruling that unlike its older
streetcars, Washington's PCCs could be run with a
single operator.

Capital Transit's PCC livery was a rather
restrained blue-green and gray. But that changed
as part of a big shakeup. Antagonized by the new
hard-line owner of Capital Transit, the federal
government revoked its franchise and awarded it
in 1956 to an entrepreneur named O. Roy Chalk, on
the condition that the streetcars would be replaced
with buses by 1963. Chalk fought for the PCCs,
experimentally air-conditioning one and proposing
innovative services.

Chalk renamed the system D.C. Transit and
tucked it into his business empire as a subsidiary of
Trans Caribbean Airways. He painted up his transit
vehicles in a tropical theme, and even installed Trans
Caribbean Airways counters in DC Transit ticket
offices, rather like offering Virgin America tickets at
Muni Metro stations.

Despite Chalk's efforts, D.C. Transit foundered
financially and was taken over by the government,
like virtually every other transit system, with
streetcars disappearing from Washington in 1962.
But the livery lives on with car No. 1076, right down
to the decal by the front door saying, "An Affiliate of
Trans Caribbean Airways."

builder
St. Louis Car Co., 1946

modifier
Brookville Equipment Co., 2004

seats
50

weight
37,600 lb. (17,060 kg)

length
46'5" (14.1m)

width
9'0" (2.7m)

height
10'3" (3.1m)

motors
four General Electric 1220

trucks
B-2

brakes
electric

Jeremy Whiteman photo

On F-line

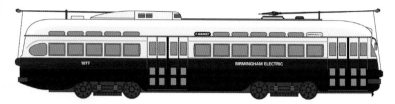

BIRMINGHAM

builder
St. Louis Car Co., 1947

modifier
Brookville Equipment Co., 2004

seats
50

weight
37,600 lb. (17,060 kg)

length
46'5" (14.1m)

width
9'0" (2.7m)

height
10'3" (3.1m)

motors
four General Electric 1220

trucks
B-2

brakes
electric

Jeremy Whiteman photo

On F-line

Built in 1947 for Twin City Rapid Transit Co., Minneapolis-St. Paul, Minnesota.
Served Minneapolis-St. Paul from 1947-53.
Served Newark, New Jersey from 1953-2001.
Purchased by Muni in 2004.
Painted in tribute to Birmingham, Alabama.

This car's exterior commemorates Birmingham, Alabama, which operated PCC streetcars from 1947 to 1953.

When streetcars were a new technology, around the turn of the 20th century, it was common for systems to be owned by the local electric utility. Electric utilities usually had the financial capacity to handle the capital outlay involved with building streetcar lines and, of course, could supply electricity to run the car at its cost, increasing the profit of the transit lines.

So it was in Birmingham, one of only two southern cities (with Dallas) to operate the streamlined PCC car. Birmingham Electric Company (BEC) was a member of the industry group that created the PCC in the 1930s, but chose to rebuild some of its existing cars rather than buy PCCs right away. At the end of World War II, BEC's streetcar fleet was made up of 27 different types of streetcars, some dating back to 1901, and almost all worn out by heavy wartime ridership.

The company ordered 48 new Pullman-Standard PCCs, which arrived in 1947. They were used on the lines that served steel mills, which generated heavy loads at shift change times especially. Streetcar lines with lighter patronage were slated for conversion to trolley buses or motor coaches. To take advantage of the PCCs' higher speeds, BEC ran them as expresses during rush hours on some routes, complementing them with buses for local service on that part of the route.

Like other transit properties in the South of that era, Birmingham's PCCs were segregated. Signs separating blacks and whites were mounted on seat backs. In December 1955, just 90 miles from Birmingham in the state capital of Montgomery, Rosa Parks famously initiated the beginning of the end of transit segregation by refusing to give up her bus seat to a white passenger. By then, however, Birmingham's PCCs were in Toronto. A new owner, who didn't have the incentive an electric company did to operate electric-powered transit, junked the streetcar system in 1953 and sold all the PCCs.

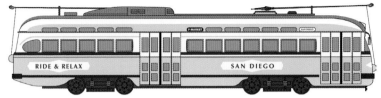

RIDE & RELAX

SAN DIEGO

**Built in 1946 for Twin City Rapid Transit Co.,
Minneapolis-St. Paul, Minnesota.
Served Minneapolis-St. Paul from 1946-53.
Served Newark, New Jersey from 1953-2001.
Purchased by Muni in 2004.
Painted in tribute to San Diego, California.**

This streetcar is painted to honor San Diego, which operated PCC streetcars from 1937 to 1949, and again starting in 2011.

San Diego Electric Railway (SDER) was originally owned by the sons of San Francisco 'Sugar King' Claus Spreckels. They also owned the famed Hotel del Coronado and the San Diego & Arizona Railroad. In the mid-1930s, SDER's fleet featured heavy, roomy conventional streetcars, built in 1923, that were generally popular with riders, along with older wooden cars. Not standing pat, SDER became the first west coast operator of PCCs in the spring of 1937, beating out Los Angeles by a few weeks.

San Diego's 28 PCCs were concentrated on a few lines. After the end of World War II, the city's population exploded, with many developments beyond the reach of the streetcar lines. In 1948, the system was sold to a former executive of National City Lines, who followed their familiar playbook of bus conversion. Rail service was abandoned in 1949. Twenty of the PCCs were sold to El Paso; the rest couldn't find a buyer and were sold to a scrapper eight years later. Two of those cars ended up being preserved.

But in 1981, San Diego started the American streetcar renaissance with its bright red 'San Diego Trolley', actually light rail vehicles, running on old railroad right-of-way from downtown to the Mexican border. The system has steadily expanded across the region and, in 2011, added a PCC car (formerly Muni No. 1123) in weekend service on a downtown loop called the 'Silver Line', painted in a version of the original San Diego PCC livery.

One note on the paint scheme of No. 1078. San Diego's original PCC livery included painted signs promoting the "Zoo and Balboa Park via lines 7 and 11." Well, San Francisco has a zoo and a Balboa Park too, but lines with those numbers don't take you there. So some of the wording on the painted signs has been modified. But the trademark message "Ride & Relax" is still there to see.

SAN DIEGO

builder
St. Louis Car Co., 1946

modifier
Brookville Equipment Co., 2004

seats
50

weight
37,600 lb. (17,060 kg)

length
46'5" (14.1m)

width
9'0" (2.7m)

height
10'3" (3.1m)

motors
four General Electric 1220

trucks
B-2

brakes
electric

Jeremy Whiteman photo

On F-line

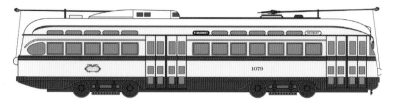

builder
St. Louis Car Co., 1946

modifier
Brookville Equipment Co., 2004

seats
50

weight
37,600 lb. (17,060 kg)

length
46'5" (14.1m)

width
9'0" (2.7m)

height
10'3" (3.1m)

motors
four General Electric 1220

trucks
B-2

brakes
electric

Built in 1946 for Twin City Rapid Transit Co., Minneapolis-St. Paul, Minnesota.
Served Minneapolis-St. Paul from 1946-53.
Served Newark, New Jersey from 1953-2001.
Purchased by Muni in 2004.
Painted in tribute to Detroit, Michigan.

This car's exterior commemorates Detroit, which operated PCC streetcars from 1947 to 1956.

While Detroit prided itself as the home of modern vehicle design, the Detroit Department of Street Railways (DSR) stayed away from the streamlined PCC streetcar when it first appeared. Instead, the city government agency (which had taken over a private operator in 1922) tinkered incessantly with its huge fleet of boxy 'Peter Witt' streetcars—781 in all—trying to make them faster and quieter, with little success.

When they did briefly consider buying PCCs in 1939, the city decided against it, both because they believed streetcars would soon be obsolete and because the carmen's union rejected the idea of operating streetcars with a single crew member.

After World War II, the carmen's union relented on its insistence on two-person crews. Detroit changed its mind and bought 186 new PCCs, delivered in 1947 and 1949. They were put to work mainly on the heavy Woodward, Michigan, and Jefferson lines. Like other metropolitan areas, though, migration to the suburbs put more and more people out of streetcar range. Perhaps influenced by Detroit's automobile culture, the city council in 1954 approved the abandonment of two major lines if a buyer could be found for the almost new PCCs.

San Francisco outbid Mexico City for 80 of the Detroit PCCs, but after San Francisco's financial problems killed the deal, almost all Detroit's PCCs went to Mexico City. The last line, Woodward Avenue, closed in April 1956, making Detroit an all-bus operation (although the Department of Street Railways didn't get around to changing its name to the Detroit Department of Transportation for almost twenty years).

A new Woodward Avenue line, using modern streetcars and called the QLine, is scheduled for opening in 2017.

And every day, San Francisco pays tribute to the streetcar past of the 'Motor City' in the tan and red livery of the Detroit Department of Street Railways gracing car No. 1079.

Adolfo Echeverry photo

On F-line

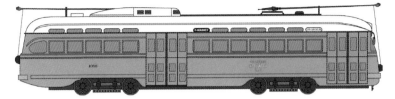

Built in 1946 for Twin City Rapid Transit Co.,
Minneapolis-St. Paul, Minnesota.
Served Minneapolis-St. Paul from 1946-53.
Served Newark, New Jersey from 1953-2001.
Purchased by Muni in 2004.
Painted in tribute to Los Angeles, California.

This car is painted in the livery of Los Angeles
Transit Lines (LATL), which operated PCC streetcars
after World War II. Los Angeles Railway (whose 1937
PCC livery is worn by Muni No. 1052) sold out in
1945 to National City Lines (NCL), which was owned
by oil, tire, and bus companies. NCL was infamous
for buying up streetcar lines and converting them
to buses, to the profit of its owners (who were
convicted of federal conspiracy charges in 1949).
However, NCL didn't follow its normal script in
LA. Operating as Los Angeles Transit Lines, NCL
actually bought more streetcars, forty extra-wide
PCCs of No. 1080's body style in 1948, to modernize
the P-Pico line, where patronage was too heavy
for buses. Some other streetcar lines also survived,
possibly because of the superb maintenance of
the streetcars, track, and overhead wire, which Los
Angeles Railway had kept up, even as other systems
around the country fell into disrepair.

The new Pico line streetcars were painted in the
standard NCL paint scheme modeled on this car.
NCL streetcars in other cities, such as El Paso, wore
nearly identical liveries (Muni's No. 1073 wears a
later El Paso livery). If the East Bay's Key System
had gone ahead with a potential PCC purchase, you
would have seen this livery in Oakland, too.

Massive freeway construction in the 1950s and
the resulting suburban sprawl stole riders from both
LATL and its interurban counterpart, Pacific Electric.
Six major LATL streetcar lines were converted to
buses in 1955. This allowed PCCs to take over from
the last of the company's conventional streetcars on
such lines as the crosstown V-Vermont-Vernon and
the S-San Pedro-West Eighth Street.

In 1958, publicly owned Los Angeles Metropolitan
Transit Authority (LAMTA) took over LATL and
repainted its PCCs in a handsome two-tone green
and white livery. But it only lasted a few years.
Despite daily ridership of 40,000 on the Pico line,
almost twice what the crowded F-line handles
today in San Francisco, PCCs disappeared from Los
Angeles in 1963 and automobile domination of the
southland was complete.

But now, rail is undergoing a renaissance in Los
Angeles, with both heavy-rail subway and light rail
lines slowly spreading across the region—still a pale
shadow of the Southland's streetcar systems of
yore, but a new beginning nevertheless.

builder
St. Louis Car Co., 1946

modifier
Brookville Equipment Co., 2004

seats
50

weight
37,600 lb. (17,060 kg)

length
46'5" (14.1m)

width
9'0" (2.7m)

height
10'3" (3.1m)

motors
four General Electric 1220

trucks
B-2

brakes
electric

Jeremy Whiteman photo

At Muni Metro East Yard

Timeline: Cable Cars in SF

1873—Andrew Hallidie opens world's first
cable car line on Clay Street

1878—California Street Cable Railroad opens;
portions remain in service today

1883—Cable cars begin operating on Market Street

1887—First practical electric streetcars run in Richmond, Virginia,
supplanting cable cars as 'state-of-the-art' transit technology

1888—Powell Street Railway Co. opens cable lines
on Powell, Mason, Washington, and Jackson Streets;
portions remain in service today

1891—Last all-new cable car line opens
on O'Farrell, Jones, and Hyde Streets;
most of Hyde Street segment remains in service today

1906—Earthquake and fire devastate San Francisco;
aided by bribes, United Railroads converts
Market Street cable lines to electric streetcars

1909—City buys Geary Street cable car line; converts it
to first Municipal Railway (Muni) streetcar lines in 1912

1941—Castro Street cable car line closes

1942—Sacramento-Clay cable car line,
including world's first cable route, closes

1944—Muni acquires Powell Street cable car lines as
part of takeover of private Market Street Railway Company

1947—Grassroots citizens' campaign, led by
Friedel Klussmann, defeats plan of Mayor Roger Lapham
to convert Powell Street cable lines to buses

1952—Muni begins operating cable car lines on California,
Hyde, and Jones Streets, acquired from bankrupt
California Street Cable Railroad

1954—Following intense battle, SF voters narrowly agree to
'consolidate' cable car system, cutting route mileage in half

1957—Powell-Hyde line opens, combining segments
of two old lines; last remaining cable car outside
San Francisco, in Dunedin, New Zealand, closes

1964—Cable cars declared a National Historic Landmark

1965—Women allowed to ride on cable car steps for first time

1982—In decrepit condition, cable car system shut down
for complete rebuilding; reopens 1984

1998—Fannie Mae Barnes becomes first
female cable car 'gripman'

In today's world of fads and copies, San Francisco boasts an original. There is nothing else exactly like the cable cars anywhere in the world.

Cable cars were invented here in 1873, dominated the city's transit scene for more than thirty years, were almost extinguished by the 1906 Earthquake and Fire, soldiered on through two World Wars as a quaint relic (even then), survived an assassination attempt by misguided (or malicious) politicians in the late 1940s, were wounded in a follow-up assault in the 1950s, but survived it all to become a worldwide symbol of San Francisco.

Today, they are one of two National Historic Landmarks that move (New Orleans' St. Charles streetcar line is the other), and both their continued operation and minimum level of service are locked into San Francisco's City Charter. Their history is a fascinating amalgam of technology, politics, and passion. Here, we concentrate on the basics of the current system.

Today, there are two types of cable cars in regular service. Though they differ in appearance, their operation is almost identical.

The California Street cable car line uses twelve larger, maroon cable cars that have an open seating section at each end and a closed section in the middle. These cars can be operated from either end, and turn around by means of a simple switch at the end of the line.

The two Powell Street lines (Powell-Hyde & Powell-Mason) use smaller cable cars, operable from only one end. They thus require turntables to reverse direction at the ends of the lines. There are 28 Powell cars kept on the roster at any given time. Several sport historic liveries recapturing the look of the cars at various points in the twelve-decade history of the service.

Additionally, there are unique cable cars from now-vanished lines that Market Street Railway is working to return to service in the future.

California St. Cable Cars

CALIFORNIA STREET CABLE CAR ROSTER

No. 49
Built 1992 by Muni

No. 50*
Built 1910 by Cal Cable

No. 51*
Built 1906 by Holman

No. 52
Built 1996 by Muni

No. 53*
Built 1907 by Holman

No. 54
Built 1907 by Holman

No. 55
Retired

No. 56*
Built 1913 by Cal Cable

No. 57
Built 1914 by Cal Cable

No. 58*
Built 1914 by Cal Cable

No. 59
Built 1998 by Muni

No. 60
Built 2003 by Muni

* Served the O'Farrell, Jones & Hyde line until 1954

seats
68 (34 seated, 34 standing)

weight
16,800 lb. (7,620 kg)

length
30'3" (9.2m)

width
8'0" (2.4m)

height
10'2" (3.1m)

track gauge
3'6" (1.07m)

Today's California Street cable cars are modeled on a design introduced in 1891 by the California Street Cable Railroad Company (Cal Cable). This design featured a closed center section flanked by open sections on each end. The car could be operated from either end, thus not requiring a turntable or turning loop. This 'California type' design was widely adopted throughout the western U.S. for both cable cars and streetcars and was used in San Francisco for half a century as the standard streetcar design.

Cal Cable's original fleet was completely destroyed in the 1906 Earthquake and Fire. The company built new cable cars much like the originals but with corner posts and windows on the ends for greater strength.

In 1952, Muni took over the financially insolvent Cal Cable. After a ferocious political fight, voters approved a realignment of Muni's cable car system that cut the length of the California line in half, while the O'Farrell, Jones & Hyde line and the Powell line that ran along Washington and Jackson Streets to Pacific Heights were discontinued in favor of a new Powell-Hyde line that used pieces of each.

The best cable cars from both the California and O'Farrell, Jones & Hyde lines were kept and repainted for the truncated California St. line, which reopened in 1957. The livery of these cable cars has changed little since this type was first built following the 1906 Earthquake: predominantly maroon, with distinctive 'ribbons' on the ends describing the route served by the cable car. When the entire cable car system was rebuilt in 1982-84, Muni changed the owner's panel at the bottom of the sides to light blue, giving these double-end cars some resemblance to the livery that the single-end Powell cable cars received at the same time.

This special double-end cable car was built in 1906 by W. L. Holman & Company, which also built the San Francisco Municipal Railway's first streetcars. It served the O'Farrell, Jones & Hyde line until that route was discontinued in 1954.

Like many identical surplus cable cars, it was sold, but found a wonderful caretaker in Mr. H. Stanley Brown, a cattle rancher from Santa Barbara County. He built rails through his ranch, motorized the cable car, and used it to give prospective cattle buyers tours of his herd.

Protected under cover, the car remained in good condition until Brown's family donated it to Market Street Railway—Muni's nonprofit preservation partner— in 1993. After extensive cosmetic restoration by its volunteers, Market Street Railway donated it to Muni, which restored it to operating condition. Car No. 42 reentered San Francisco service after a half-century absence in 2005, carrying mayors from around the world on California and Hyde Streets as part of the United Nations' World Environment Day. It serves today as the mayor's ceremonial cable car and carries passengers on the California Street line during special heritage events.

On September 24, 2016, to celebrate the 125th anniversary year of cable car service on Hyde Street, Car No. 42 carried invited guests on a ceremonial run down Hyde Street to the famous Buena Vista Café and Ghirardelli Square and back to the carbarn, the first time a cable car in O'Farrell, Jones & Hyde livery had carried passengers on the Hyde Street hill since 1954.

builder
W. L. Holman & Co., 1906

seats
60 (29 seated, 31 standing)

weight
15,500 lb. (7,030 kg)

length
27'6" (8.4m)

width
8'0" (2.4m)

height
10'5" (3.2m)

track gauge
3'6" (1.07m)

Powell St. Cable Cars

POWELL STREET STANDARD LIVERY CABLE CAR ROSTER

No. 2 built 1893 by Carter

No. 4 built 1994 by Muni

No. 5 built 1893 by Carter

No. 6 built 1893 by Carter

No. 7 built 1893 by Carter

No. 8 retired

No. 10 built 1893 by Carter

No. 11 built 1893 by Carter

No. 14 built 1963 by Muni

No. 17 built 1887 by Mahoney

No. 18 built 1962 by Muni

No. 19 built 1986 by Muni

No. 20 built 1893 by Carter

No. 21 built 1992 by Muni

No. 22 built 1887 by Mahoney

No. 23 built 1890 by FCH

No. 24 built 1887 by Mahoney

No. 27 built 1887 by Mahoney

No. 28 built 2004 by Muni

seats
60 (29 seated, 31 standing)

weight
15,500 lb. (7,030 kg)

length
27'6" (8.4m)

width
8'0" (2.4m)

height
10'5" (3.2m)

track gauge
3'6" (1.07m)

Today's Powell Street cable car fleet consists of a mix of original cable cars and those more recently constructed to the same exacting standards by Muni craftsworkers.

When the Powell-Mason cable line first opened in 1888, it used cable cars that looked almost exactly like today's. That original fleet was destroyed in the 1906 Earthquake and Fire, but a group of identical cable cars used on the Sacramento-Clay line escaped the fire, and was moved over to the Powell line. So whenever you see a Powell cable car dated before 1906, remember it started its career on the Sacramento-Clay line. The original builders of this fleet included Carter Brothers of Newark, California, a subcontractor of Mahoney Bros. in San Francisco, and the Ferries & Cliff House Railway shops.

The Powell Street cable car fleet was generally well maintained through the decades by its various owners, but inevitably wood rots and metal rusts. It is a testimony to the cable car builders that the little cars have soldiered on so long with the jarring stops, lurching starts, and crush loads they're often subjected to.

Since Muni took over the Powell cable cars in 1944, there has been an almost continuous program of rebuilding the cars. At first, just the worst pieces of wood and metal were replaced. Then came a period when the old roofs were salvaged and much of the car beneath was completely rebuilt. Then, some cable cars were built almost entirely new. Today, Muni pursues all three of these strategies to keep the Powell Street cable car fleet on the street and up to strength. All the cars in the fleet built before Muni took over have been heavily rebuilt by Muni craftsworkers, usually twice, since then.

This page lists the Powell cable cars that appear in the standard maroon and blue livery adopted in 1984 (actually a modified version of the original 1888 livery). Subsequent pages showcase Powell Street cable cars wearing liveries of the past. At different times, Powell cable cars were predominantly yellow, red, blue, and green. All these liveries are represented today, thanks to the great work of Muni's cable car painters, with support from Muni's nonprofit preservation partner, Market Street Railway.

One other Powell cable car painted in this livery graces the promenade in center field at AT&T Park. Retired Powell car No. 4 was made No. 44 to honor the great Willie McCovey, for whom the waterway just beyond is also named.

Livery: 1888-1893   No. 1

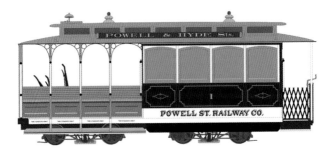

This car wears the original 1888 Powell Street Railway Company livery. It was first applied to this car in 1973, as part of the celebration of the centennial of the world's first cable car line, which ran on Clay Street.

The maroon and sky blue livery on this car was so popular with the public that Muni decided to repaint the rest of the Powell fleet in a simplified version of it when the cable car system was rebuilt in 1982-84. Powell Car No. 1 gradually lost some of its distinctiveness during repairs and repainting in subsequent decades, but in 2014 emerged with its ornate details restored, with help from Market Street Railway. It is considered the flagship of the Powell Street fleet.

builder
San Francisco Municipal Railway, 1973

seats
60 (29 seated, 31 standing)

weight
15,500 lb. (7,030 kg)

length
27'6" (8.4m)

width
8'0" (2.4m)

height
10'5" (3.2m)

track gauge
3'6" (1.07m)

Livery: 1893-1905   No. 15

This car displays the livery that Powell-Mason cable cars wore from 1893 to around 1905 under the Market Street Railway Co., whose Powell-Mason cable cars were painted yellow with red trim.

United Railroads took over the Powell Street cable lines in 1902, and this yellow livery disappeared from the Powell-Mason cable cars by 1905, but returned on cable car No. 15 in 2009, when it was constructed virtually from scratch by Muni craftsworkers to enter service.

This piece of 21st century craftsmanship is a fitting tribute to the 19th century Powell-Mason line, which today is the oldest surviving transit line in America still operating its original route with its original type of equipment.

builder
San Francisco Municipal Railway, 2009

seats
60 (29 seated, 31 standing)

weight
15,500 lb. (7,030 kg)

length
27'6" (8.4m)

width
8'0" (2.4m)

height
10'5" (3.2m)

track gauge
3'6" (1.07m)

Livery: 1902-1909

builder
Ferries & Cliff House
Railway, 1890

seats
60 (29 seated, 31 standing)

weight
15,500 lb. (7,030 kg)

length
27'6" (8.4m)

width
8'0" (2.4m)

height
10'5" (3.2m)

track gauge
3'6" (1.07m)

The fiery red of this cable car is a reminder that Powell St. cable cars were painted this way on the day they went up in flames in the 1906 Earthquake and Fire. By 1905, United Railroads (URR) had painted all its Powell cable cars red with gray roofs. The Earthquake and Fire destroyed virtually the entire Powell St. cable car fleet. To replace the Powell St. fleet, URR used cable cars, including this one, that had been on the Sacramento-Clay line and were stored outside the fire zone.

By about 1909, the transferred red cable cars were repainted green, modeled on Powell cable car No. 13.

Livery: 1907-early 1920s

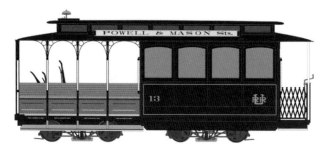

builder
San Francisco
Municipal Railway, 1991

seats
60 (29 seated, 31 standing)

weight
15,500 lb. (7,030 kg)

length
27'6" (8.4m)

width
8'0" (2.4m)

height
10'5" (3.2m)

track gauge
3'6" (1.07m)

This cable car is painted in the livery adopted by United Railroads (URR) in the aftermath of the 1906 Earthquake and Fire. Virtually the entire Powell St. cable car fleet was incinerated along with the car barn and powerhouse at Washington & Mason Streets. However, more than two dozen identical cable cars serving the Sacramento-Clay route survived and were shifted over to the Powell St. lines when the powerhouse was rebuilt in 1907. The 'new' Powell St. cable cars were repainted green with red trim, as were other URR cable cars and streetcars.

With this post-Earthquake livery, modeled today on car No. 13, green became the base color for Powell St. cable cars for more than three-quarters of a century.

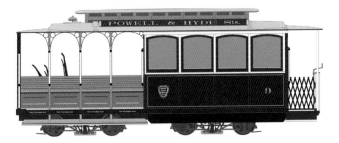

This cable car is painted in the first version of the 'White Front' livery of Market Street Railway Company (MSRy), worn by Powell St. cable cars from about 1927 until the Municipal Railway took over the Powell St. lines in 1944.

There were several generations of companies named Market Street Railway. This version took over the transit lines operated by United Railroads (URR) in 1921. A well-run but frugal outfit, MSRy retained the basic URR green paint scheme it inherited, but in 1927 started painting the ends of its cable cars and streetcars white as a patented safety measure. Car No. 9 displays the initial version of this scheme, featuring red window sashes.

builder
San Francisco
Municipal Railway, 1997

seats
60 (29 seated, 31 standing)

weight
15,500 lb. (7,030 kg)

length
27'6" (8.4m)

width
8'0" (2.4m)

height
10'5" (3.2m)

track gauge
3'6" (1.07m)

Livery: 1937-1944   No. 12

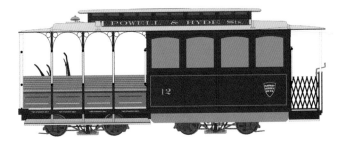

As the Depression lingered on, the private Market Street Railway Company did everything it could to save money. This included simplifying the paint schemes of its streetcars and cable cars. It took longer for painters to add different paint colors around the windows, so starting in 1937, the ends of cars were painted solid white and the sides solid green; no special trim color for windows. This simplest cable car livery ever is modeled on Car No. 12, which was heavily rebuilt by Muni's cable car carpentry shop in 2016. It represents an era when austerity ruled on the streets of San Francisco.

builder
Carter Brothers, 1893

seats
60 (29 seated, 31 standing)

weight
15,500 lb. (7,030 kg)

length
27'6" (8.4m)

width
8'0" (2.4m)

height
10'5" (3.2m)

track gauge
3'6" (1.07m)

Livery: 1944-1946

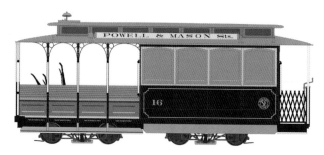

builder
San Francisco
Municipal Railway, 1990

seats
60 (29 seated, 31 standing)

weight
15,500 lb. (7,030 kg)

length
27'6" (8.4m)

width
8'0" (2.4m)

height
10'5" (3.2m)

track gauge
3'6" (1.07m)

When it bought out Market Street Railway Co. in 1944, the San Francisco Municipal Railway's official colors for its streetcars and buses were blue with yellow trim. Muni painted two Powell cable cars into this scheme (today's Nos. 3 and 10).

However, this repainting project stalled and Muni soon reverted to Market Street Railway Co's green as its primary fleet color, with cream fronts and trim, a color scheme that also adorned all new Muni streetcars and buses for 25 years.

But the blue and gold (actually yellow) livery represents an important period in Muni history, and so is represented in the Powell Street cable car fleet by No. 16.

Livery: 1946-early 1960s

builder
Ferries & Cliff House
Railway, 1890

seats
60 (29 seated, 31 standing)

weight
15,500 lb. (7,030 kg)

length
27'6" (8.4m)

width
8'0" (2.4m)

height
10'5" (3.2m)

track gauge
3'6" (1.07m)

The first of several variations of Muni's long-time green and cream paint scheme started appearing on Powell St. cable cars in 1946. The next year, Mayor Roger Lapham tried to scrap the Powell cable car system in favor of buses, but he was stopped by civic outrage orchestrated by the famed 'cable car lady', Friedel Klussmann.

In the green and cream era, which lasted 36 years, the owner's panel on the lower sides of the Powell cars was first lettered "Municipal Railway", as on this car. In 1949, Powell car No. 524 was sent to the Chicago Railroad Fair with the owner's panel lettered "Municipal Railway of San Francisco", presumably to ensure people knew its home city. In the early 1960s, other Powell cars received similar San Francisco Municipal Railway lettering (see car No. 3).

The green and cream livery of cable car No. 3 evolved from the original livery (seen on No. 26) introduced by Muni in 1946, three years after it took over the Powell lines with the purchase of Market Street Railway Company. The original livery coincided with the attempt by Mayor Roger Lapham to scrap the Powell cables in favor of buses. Lapham's plan was resoundingly beaten by civic activists led by Friedel Klussmann. In tribute to her, car No. 3 was left in the green and cream livery when all the other Powell St. cars were repainted maroon and light blue during the rebuilding of 1982-84. Car No. 3 carried a plaque dedicating it to Mrs. Klussmann, subsequently transferred to Powell car No. 1.

builder
Carter Brothers, 1893

seats
60 (29 seated, 31 standing)

weight
15,500 lb. (7,030 kg)

length
27'6" (8.4m)

width
8'0" (2.4m)

height
10'5" (3.2m)

track gauge
3'6" (1.07m)

Cable Car Powerhouse and Museum

Since the Powell cable line first opened in 1888, its cable cars have been stored and serviced in the same building that houses the cable car machinery—the giant wheels and motors that make the cars move. It's open to the public with free admission. A museum with antique cable cars and displays, along with a gift shop, occupies the balcony overlooking the powerhouse. The cable car maintenance and storage area above is closed to the public.

1201 Mason Street (corner of Washington), where the Powell-Mason and Powell-Hyde cable lines come together.

Open every day, 10:00am - 5:00pm (6:00pm in summer).

More information at cablecarmuseum.org, or by calling (415) 474-1887.

STREETCAR RIDING TIPS

San Francisco's historic streetcars have become immensely popular with visitors and residents alike. They are often crowded, although less so than the cable cars during visitor season. These tips will help you get the most enjoyment from your trip.

Ride at less crowded times
While the streetcars run continuously from 6am until after midnight every day, some times are less crowded than others, making for a more pleasant ride. During visitor season (June to September), try riding between 9am and noon or between 6pm and 9pm weekdays. Weekends can be crowded year-round; if you ride before noon, you'll have a better chance of getting a seat.

Ride the less crowded part of the line
If you're primarily interested in the streetcar ride itself, rather than a specific destination, the stretch of the line from Fifth Street west to Castro is less crowded and passes through interesting San Francisco neighborhoods.

Board at less crowded stops
Some stops draw big crowds, while the adjacent stop just a block away is less crowded. Bound for Fisherman's Wharf from Powell and Market? We suggest using the Fifth Street F-line stop rather than the more crowded stop at Fourth Street. Wharf-bound from the Ferry Building? If the Ferry Terminal stop is crowded, walk one-half block south (toward the Bay Bridge) and follow the tracks where they turn inland. The stop there, at our San Francisco Railway Museum (Steuart Street), is much less crowded, giving you a better shot at a seat. Leaving the Wharf for Downtown, the terminal at Jones and Beach Street is the best place to get a seat, as the streetcars often fill up at the Stockton (Pier 39) stop.

Ride in the less crowded part of the streetcar
Often, the back of the streetcar has considerably more room than the front.

Have fare ready
If you're planning on riding for several days, or mixing multiple cable car rides with your streetcar rides, we recommend buying a Muni Passport (see p.5). If you plan just a couple streetcar rides, paying with cash is cheaper. The current fare is posted on signs on poles at each stop. Keep an eye out for them. Have exact fare ready. Operators do not carry change.

READ ABOUT RIDING THE

CABLE CAR RIDING TIPS

Many people now dismiss our city's cable cars as a Disneyland-type attraction. And when you see the frequently long lines at the turntables of the Powell Street lines, it's understandable. But it's also a mistake. Follow these tips and you'll enjoy our cable cars the way savvy San Franciscans do.

Ride the Powell lines early
If you want to experience cable cars as they operated before they were a tourist magnet, come as early in the morning as you can. Boarding before 8am, you'll share the cable car with San Francisco commuters and avoid lines. Grab a coffee when you get to your destination and enjoy some serenity at the start of the day.

Try getting on at O'Farrell Street
Usually, the Powell cable cars leave Market Street with room for a few more riders. If the line at the turntable is long and you're determined to ride a Powell car, you can walk up two blocks from the turntable to the corner of O'Farrell Street and try boarding at the stop there. This doesn't always work, but it's worth a try.

Ride the California line
If the lines for the Powell cars look daunting, grab an F-line streetcar and get off at the California Street cable car stop (Drumm Street.) There is hardly ever a wait on the California line. You won't go around curves, but you'll get a great ride through the Financial District and Chinatown and over historic Nob Hill without a long wait.

Take the Powell-Mason line from the Wharf
In the Wharf area, there are two cable car turntables. Both lines end up at the same place, Powell & Market Streets. The line for the Powell-Hyde line at Hyde & Beach Streets (near Ghirardelli Square) is usually longer than the line for the Powell-Mason line at Bay & Taylor Streets.

Buy a Muni Passport
If you're planning on taking a round-trip cable car ride along with an F-line round-trip, a Muni Passport gives you the best value. Cable cars do not accept or issue transfers so you have to pay a full fare every time you board. The Muni Passport avoids that and is also good on Muni buses and the Muni Metro subway (but not BART). There are 1-, 3-, and 7-day versions of the Muni Passport. A partial list of places to buy them can be found on p.5.

'STEEL TRIANGLE' ON PAGE 6.

Ride History to See History

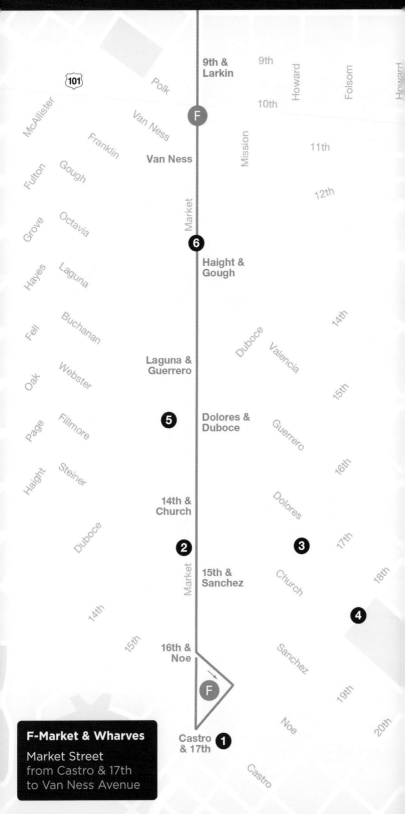

F-Market & Wharves

Market Street from Castro & 17th to Van Ness Avenue

What's Outside as You Ride?

The historic streetcars of the F-line carry you past some of San Francisco's most historic sites. Here's a selection of history-related spots on or near the F-line, starting at the Castro end of the line to the Fisherman's Wharf terminal. If you're traveling from the Wharf, read this section backwards!

Market St., from Castro & 17th to Van Ness Ave...

1. Castro Street and Castro Theatre
Castro Street had a cable car line until 1941. Today, the 'Castro' is America's most famous gay neighborhood. Local landmarks include Harvey Milk's camera store at 575 Castro, near 19th Street, and the 1922 Castro Theater, whose neon marquee defines the neighborhood.

2. Swedish-American Hall
This 1907 building at 2174 Market near Sanchez retains its original detail and recalls the days when Scandinavian immigrants lived in this part of the city. Its basement Cafe Du Nord was a notorious speakeasy during Prohibition and is now a hip bar and nightclub.

3. Mission Dolores
Located three blocks from the F-line, Mission San Francisco de Asis (commonly called Mission Dolores) honors the namesake of the city, St. Francis of Assisi. Founded in 1776, the current structure dates from 1791. It is generally open from 9am-4pm.

4. Dolores Park
F-line streetcars going to and from the car house use the J-Church streetcar line, which runs through this scenic park with stunning skyline views from the top at 20th and Church. Nearby is the Liberty Hill historic district with its wonderful Victorian homes.

5. "New" U.S. Mint
A granite crown on a serpentine outcrop, this 1937 fortress today strikes proof coins for collectors, but it was a general coinage mint until 1955. Bristling with security, it is closed to the public. Beneath it sits the facility where Market Street Railway has helped restore streetcars.

6. Art Deco Row
The F-line's PCC streetcars are some of the best examples of Art Deco industrial design, so it's fitting they pass San Francisco's biggest collection of antique stores from that period, between Haight and Page Streets.

Ride History to See History

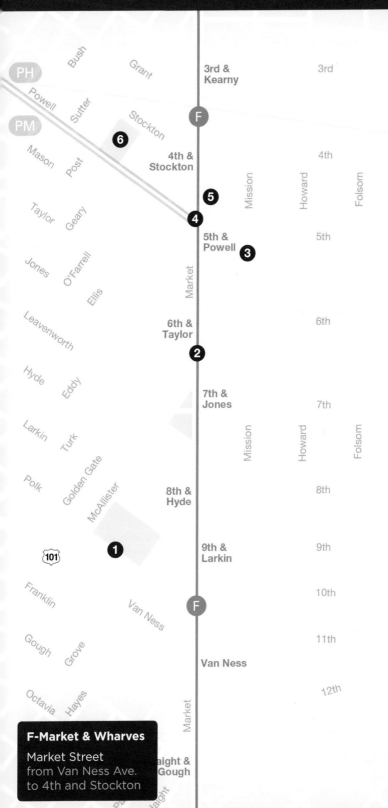

PH

PM

Bush
Grant
3rd & Kearny
3rd

Powell
Sutter
Stockton

F

Mason
Post
6

4th & Stockton
4th

Taylor
Geary
Mission
Howard
Folsom

5

4

5th & Powell
3
5th

Jones
O'Farrell
Ellis
Market

Leavenworth
6th & Taylor
6th

Hyde
Eddy
2

Larkin
Turk
7th & Jones
7th
Mission
Howard
Folsom

Polk
Golden Gate
McAllister
8th & Hyde
8th

101
1
9th & Larkin
9th

Franklin
Van Ness
10th

F

Gough
Grove
11th

Octavia
Hayes
Van Ness

Market

aight &
Gough

12th

Haight

F-Market & Wharves

Market Street
from Van Ness Ave.
to 4th and Stockton

What's Outside as You Ride?

Continuing our catalogue of historic sites visible from the windows of your F-line streetcar as you ride along.

Market Street, from Van Ness Avenue to Fourth and Stockton Streets...

1. Civic Center National Historic Landmark District
America's greatest collection of municipal buildings is highlighted by the magnificent 1915 Beaux-Arts City Hall, capped by the fifth largest dome in the world. The spectacular rotunda is open to the public Monday through Friday, and is three blocks from the F-line (Van Ness or Seventh Street stops).

2. Mid-Market
The stretch of Market between Seventh and Fifth Streets features many landmark buildings erected in the years after the 1906 Earthquake, including numerous cinemas. Economically struggling for decades, there are efforts to make it an arts district.

3. "Old" U.S. Mint
A half block south from the Fifth Street F-line stop is the "old" U.S. Mint, a Greek Revival structure opened in 1874. It was saved from destruction in the 1906 Earthquake and Fire through heroic efforts by its workers. At the time, its vaults held one-third of U.S. gold reserves.

4. Powell St. Cable Car Turntable and Flood Building
Cable cars have reversed here since 1888. Since 1904, the Flood Building has stood guard over the turntable. The floors above street level retain their original interior, unchanged from the days in the 1920s when Dashiell Hammett worked here as a Pinkerton detective.

5. Emporium Façade
Facing the Flood Building on the south side of Market is an 1896 façade by the same architect, Albert Pissis. It has fronted three successive buildings: the first was destroyed in 1906, the second was torn down in 2004 (though the monumental dome was saved) to expand a shopping mall.

6. Union Square
Two blocks north on Stockton Street sits Union Square, established in 1850 and soon named for the pro-Union rallies held there before the Civil War. Long the heart of the retail district, remodeling in 1903, 1941, and 2002 haven't altered its status as a great people-watching venue.

Ride History to See History

The Embarcadero

Ferry Terminal

(F)

Steuart

Davis

Jackson

Drumm

Steuart

Front

Washington

Spear

Battery

Clay

Main

Sansome

Sacramento

Mission

Beale

6

Main & Drumm

Montgomery

California

Fremont

5

1st & Battery

1st

Market

Kearny

Pine

Howard

Folsom

Grant

Bush

2nd

2nd & Montgomery

New Montgomery

Stockton

Sutter

4

PH

3

2 **3rd & Kearny**

3rd

Powell

PM

1

Mason

Post

4th

4th & Stockton

Taylor

Geary

(F)

Mission

Howard

Folsom

5th

5th & Powell

Market

F-Market & Wharves

Market Street
from 4th & Stockton
to Ferry Terminal

6th

What's Outside as You Ride?

A selection of historic sites on lower Market Street along the F-line.

Market Street, from Fourth and Stockton to Ferry Terminal...

1. Up From the Ashes

Between Powell Street and Second Street is a legacy of the 1906 cataclysm that wiped out downtown: a fine collection of commercial buildings that rose from the ashes in the following few years. A time traveler from a century ago would recognize this part of Market Street.

2. Newspaper Row

A century ago, the corner of Third, Kearny, Geary, and Market was the most powerful press center on the West Coast, with the *Chronicle, Examiner,* and *Call* occupying buildings on three of the four corners. All these buildings survive today.

3. Birthplace of Muni

On Geary Street, just a few feet west of Market, the first big city publicly owned transit system in America began operation on December 28, 1912, with Mayor James Rolph, Jr. personally operating Municipal Railway streetcar No. 1, still running today.

4. Palace Hotel

The Palace Hotel has occupied the corner of Market and New Montgomery streets since 1875. A king (Kalakaua of Hawaii) and a president (Warren G. Harding) died here. The original building, incinerated in 1906, was replaced by the one here today.

5. History Lost

Between Second and Beale Streets, much of Market Street's historic fabric was lost in the 1970s and 1980s as generic high-rise office buildings replaced post-1906 buildings. However, several fine period buildings and monuments survive.

6. History Preserved

Three fine historic office buildings anchor the south side of lower Market. At Main Street, the 1923 Matson Building and 1925 PG&E Building were made one structure after the 1989 earthquake. The 1915 Southern Pacific Building anchors the corner where the F-line turns onto Steuart Street.

Ride History to See History

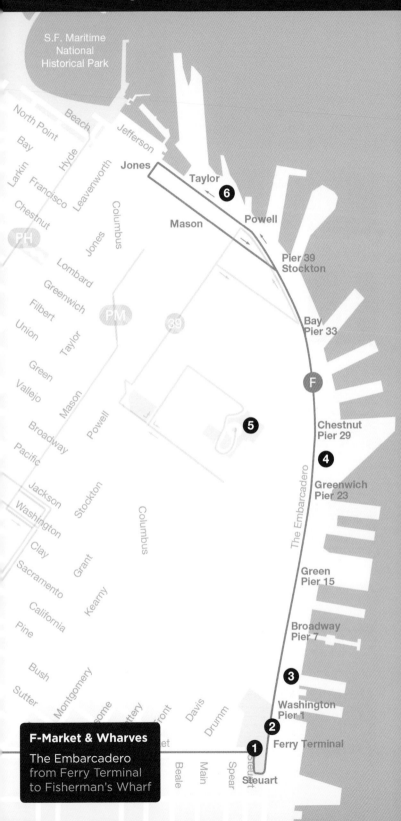

S.F. Maritime National Historical Park

Jones

Taylor

6

Powell

Mason

Pier 39
Stockton

PH

Bay
Pier 33

PM

39

F

5

Chestnut
Pier 29

4

Greenwich
Pier 23

Green
Pier 15

Broadway
Pier 7

3

Washington
Pier 1

2

Ferry Terminal

1

Steuart

The Embarcadero

F-Market & Wharves

The Embarcadero
from Ferry Terminal
to Fisherman's Wharf

What's Outside as You Ride?

Unlike Market Street, where rail transit has ruled since Civil War days, streetcars reaching Fisherman's Wharf along The Embarcadero is a 21st century phenomenon. There's still plenty of history here, though.

The Embarcadero, from the Ferry Building to Fisherman's Wharf...

1. Ferry Loop Site
The plaza area in front of the Ferry Building was once one of the busiest streetcar terminals in the world, a triple-track loop circled by hundreds of streetcars an hour serving ferry riders. See what it looked like at the San Francisco Railway Museum, just south of this site at the Steuart St. F-line stop.

2. Ferry Building
Opened in 1898, this grand structure, whose clock tower is modeled on one in Seville, Spain, was the world's second busiest transit terminal in the early 1930s (after London's Charing Cross Station). Long run-down, it was reborn in 2003 as a vibrant gourmet marketplace.

3. Riverboat Landing
From 1927 to 1940, a pair of steamboats, the *Delta Queen* and *Delta King*, carried passengers between San Francisco and Sacramento overnight. Both boats are preserved elsewhere. The passenger waiting room at Pier 1½ has been restored as a restaurant.

4. Finger Piers
Tramp steamers to Shanghai and Sydney, liners to Honolulu, vessels from near and far berthed at the finger piers north of the Ferry Building for decades. The landmark Beaux-Arts bulkhead buildings facing the street date as far back as 1918.

5. Coit Tower
A sentinel above the waterfront, this 1933 memorial to San Francisco firefighters crowns Telegraph Hill, where a semaphore alerted citizens to the arrival of ships from afar in the 19th century. See it and much more history on our ride-walk tour, page 90.

6. Fisherman's Wharf
The historic core of Fisherman's Wharf is built around the fishing harbor, which opened in 1900. Several restaurants surrounding the compact harbor bear the names of the Italian-American families that have been operating them for many decades.

Ride History to See History

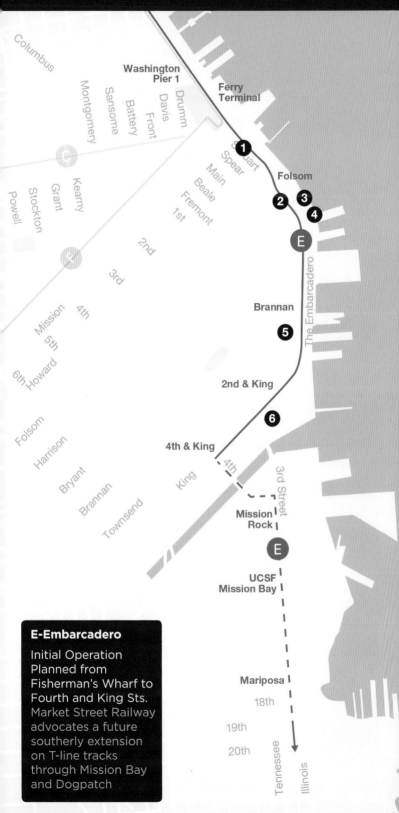

Columbus

Washington
Pier 1

Ferry
Terminal

Montgomery
Sansome
Battery
Front
Davis
Drumm
Spear
Stewart

1

Main
Beale
Fremont
1st

Folsom

2 **3**
4

E

Kearny
Grant
Stockton
Powell

2nd

3rd

Brannan

4th
Mission
5th
6th Howard

5

The Embarcadero

2nd & King

Folsom
Harrison
Bryant
Brannan
Townsend

King

4th

6

4th & King

3rd Street

**Mission
Rock**

E

**UCSF
Mission Bay**

Mariposa

Tennessee
Illinois

18th

19th

20th

E-Embarcadero

Initial Operation
Planned from
Fisherman's Wharf to
Fourth and King Sts.
Market Street Railway
advocates a future
southerly extension
on T-line tracks
through Mission Bay
and Dogpatch

What's Outside as You Ride?

The E-line will run the length of San Francisco's waterfront boulevard, The Embarcadero (Spanish for wharf). Its northern end will be shared with the F-line; you can see those trackside attractions on the previous page. This page covers the southern portion of the E-line.

NOTE: Check signs at stops to see whether the E-line is in service.

The Embarcadero, from the Ferry Building to Caltrain Depot at 4th & King...

1. Audiffred Building and Army-Navy YMCA
Two landmark buildings grace the block between Mission and Howard. The Audiffred Building (1889) and the Army-Navy YMCA building (1926) both spent most of their lives hosting services for sailors, whose needs were met in a range of waterfront businesses for decades.

2. Coffee Time
Harrison and The Embarcadero was the site of the roasting plant for Hills Bros. Coffee (1925). Now it is a mixed-use development. Combined with nearby roasting plants for Folgers, MJB, and Schilling, a heavenly coffee scent permeated the area for decades.

3. Bay Bridge
The San Francisco-Oakland Bay Bridge (1936) is one of the busiest in the world. Its western suspension span is a spectacular landmark with its X-braced silver towers. Much of historic Rincon Hill had to be cleared for its anchorage and ramps.

4. Pier 26
Pier 26 (1915) is one of only three surviving piers in the Mission Revival style. In 1934, the Longshoremen's Union organized a west coast waterfront strike here; a deadly "Bloody Thursday" clash between police and strikers on July 5 (memorialized by a sculpture at Mission and Steuart) led to a citywide general strike.

5. Oriental Warehouse
A half-block from The Embarcadero, at 650 Delancey Street, is the Oriental Bonded Warehouse (1867), the oldest structure on the southern waterfront. It has been converted into high-end condos, symbolizing the transformation of South Beach.

6. Giants' Ballpark
Not a historic structure—yet—the ballpark (2000) merits special mention both because of the care taken to create façades that honored the old brick warehouses nearby and because it helped revitalize the South Beach neighborhood.

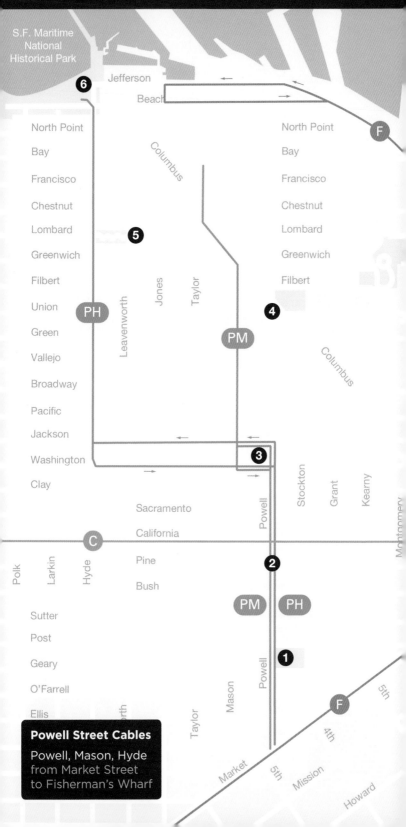

Ride History to See History

S.F. Maritime National Historical Park

Jefferson

Beach

North Point
Bay
Francisco
Chestnut
Lombard
Greenwich
Filbert
Union
Green
Vallejo
Broadway
Pacific
Jackson
Washington
Clay

Columbus

Leavenworth
Jones
Taylor

North Point
Bay
Francisco
Chestnut
Lombard
Greenwich
Filbert

Columbus

6
5
PH
4
PM
3

Stockton
Grant
Kearny

Sacramento
California
Pine
Bush

Powell

Montgomery

C

Polk
Larkin
Hyde

2

Sutter
Post
Geary
O'Farrell
Ellis

PM **PH**

Taylor
Mason
Powell

1

F

5th
4th
Mission
Howard

Market

F

Powell Street Cables

Powell, Mason, Hyde
from Market Street
to Fisherman's Wharf

What's Outside as You Ride?

The two Powell Street cable car lines share the turntable at Market and Powell Streets, then diverge to reach Fisherman's Wharf by separate routes, one through North Beach on Mason, Columbus, & Taylor, and the other over Russian Hill on Hyde Street. The Hyde line is more scenic and steep, though both have their charms.

Powell-Mason/Powell-Hyde Lines, Market to Wharf...

1. Union Square and the St. Francis Hotel
From their first day of operation in 1888, Powell cable cars have passed Union Square, which got its name in the Civil War era. The St. Francis Hotel has faced the square on Powell since 1906 and retains much of its original glory in its façade and lobby.

2. Private Clubs
The glory days of the Powell cable cars coincided with the glory days of exclusive private clubs in the city. Those days wane, but clubs survive. The Family Club (545 Powell at Bush) and the University Club (pictured, 800 Powell at California) are two handsome survivors.

3. Cable Car Museum and Powerhouse
At Washington and Mason, where the two Powell lines come together, is the cable car nerve center, originally built in 1887 and rebuilt twice. You can see how the cables are powered by giant winding wheels and visit historic displays and a gift store. Admission is free.

4. North Beach
The Powell-Mason line doesn't have the spectacular hills of the Hyde line, but it runs along the edge of the historically Italian neighborhood of North Beach, with Washington Square Park at its heart. The line runs briefly along diagonal Columbus Avenue, North Beach's "Main Street".

5. Russian Hill and 'Crookedest Street'
The Powell-Hyde line traverses Russian Hill, with its blend of homes, cafes, and stately apartment buildings. The famous twisty block of Lombard Street, actually only the second-most "crooked" street in San Francisco, was built in 1922 and swarms with tourists during the summer. San Franciscans steer clear.

6. San Francisco Maritime National Historic Park
The Hyde Street line ends in National Park land, featuring historic ships at the Hyde Street Pier, a visitor center at Jefferson and Hyde, and the Maritime Museum, a Depression Era WPA project in Art Deco design with some great period detail inside.

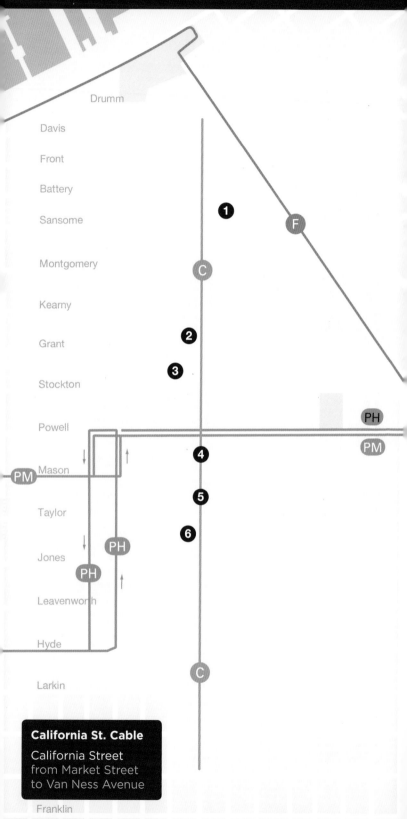

Drumm

Davis

Front

Battery

Sansome

Montgomery

Kearny

Grant

Stockton

Powell

Mason

Taylor

Jones

Leavenworth

Hyde

Larkin

California St. Cable

California Street
from Market Street
to Van Ness Avenue

Franklin

What's Outside as You Ride?

While the Powell Street cable car lines attract the most visitors, many locals in the know prefer the California Street line: less crowded, with more historic architecture and sites along the way. No curves though, and the line ends abruptly at one of the city's busiest crosstown streets, Van Ness Avenue (U.S. 101).

California St. Line from Market St. to Van Ness...

1. Financial District
Your ride starts in a canyon of skyscrapers both historic and modern. Nestled in their midst is the city's oldest restaurant, Tadich Grill, unchanged at 240 California for decades. Note the 1907 Bank of California building at Sansome, generally considered the city's finest classic banking temple.

2. Old St. Mary's
This church has stood at California Street and Grant Avenue since 1854. Built as California's first Roman Catholic cathedral, it was supplanted by a larger church in 1891, survived the earthquake but was gutted by the fire of 1906, was rebuilt, and carries on its mission as a parish church today.

3. Chinatown
The intersection of California Street and Grant Avenue also marks the heart of Chinatown. Like Old St. Mary's most of these structures were rebuilt after 1906, with much of the faux-Chinese ornamentation added to the buildings in that era. See our suggestion for a cable car/walking tour through this area on page 93.

4. Nabobs on Nob Hill
Crossing Powell Street, you enter the realm of the "nabobs" for whom Nob Hill is supposedly named. The California Street cable car line was built to serve magnates including Leland Stanford and Mark Hopkins, whose mansions gave way after 1906 to the hotels named for them between Powell and Mason.

5. Gracious Places
Nob Hill is graced with wonderful architecture. Hotels, including the Fairmont (1906), the Mark Hopkins (1925) at Mason, and the Huntington (1924) at Taylor evoke a more gracious era, as do several historic apartment buildings and the brownstone Pacific Union Club (the 1886 Flood mansion, a National Historic Landmark) at Mason.

6. Grace Cathedral
San Francisco's most famous church, the French Gothic structure went up on Charles Crocker's old mansion site beginning in 1928. It is the third largest Episcopal cathedral in the United States, with two labyrinths and numerous stained glass windows depicting famous Americans.

Combine your ride with a great walk.

Despite its hills (or perhaps because of them), San Francisco is a great walking town. The northeast quadrant of the city, where the vintage streetcars and cable cars run, is compact and historic, with surprises at every turn for both visitors and residents: a previously unseen architectural gem, a glimpse of the Bay, a new restaurant or shop.

As we've pointed out, this book is intended for San Franciscans as much as it is for our guests from around the world. Following are five ride-walk combinations highlighting San Francisco's unique history.

Photo credit: Rick Laubscher.

1 Firefighters' Tribute, Garden Stairs, and Dive Bar Jazz

Board an F-line streetcar headed toward Fisherman's Wharf at any stop. If you pay a cash fare, ask the operator for a transfer when you board. After passing the Ferry Building and starting north along The Embarcadero, look out the left side of the car to see the nozzle-shaped monument atop a rock outcrop edged with precariously placed houses. The monument is Coit Tower. (One of those houses on the edge of the precipice was home for decades to Friedel Klussmann, the woman who saved the Powell Street cable cars from extinction in 1947.)

Get off the F-line car at **Pier 39**, and wait at that same stop for the **39-Coit bus** to arrive. Show the driver your transfer and get on. (Note: you can also start this walk by getting off a Powell-Mason cable car at Union Street and walking downhill a little more than a block to Columbus Avenue. The 39-line stop you want is on eastbound Union Street just before Columbus.)

If time is tight, ask the 39-line driver to let you off at Montgomery and Union Streets. (You'll know it when you get there; it's at the top of a hill where the driver has to make a three-point turn to reverse the bus.) Walk north toward where the

street splits into upper and lower sections) two short blocks to Filbert Street. Now hang on, while we explain the longer option.

If you have more time, stay on the 39-bus while it goes back down the hill on Union, and then jogs over and up a winding street, Telegraph Hill Boulevard, to reach **Coit Tower**. Get off the bus and admire the fine Depression era murals inside the rotunda of

One of the Coit Tower murals

the tower, completed in 1933 as a memorial to San Francisco firefighters, funded by Lily Hitchcock Coit. Take the elevator to the top for great views of Alcatraz, the Golden Gate Bridge, and the city. Walk on the pathway next to the road you came up (Telegraph Hill Blvd.) until you see a street sign saying **Greenwich**. There's no actual roadway: the 'street' is the stairs going downhill.

Take the stairs to the next cross street, **Montgomery**. Turn right, but walk along the easterly (downhill) edge of the divided street one block to **Filbert**. You'll know you're there when you see a big white Art Deco building with a giant silver image on its side of a woman standing in front of the outline of California. (Bacall hosted a fugitive Bogey in her apartment here in the

1360 Montgomery, a Moderne masterpiece

From the Seat to Your Feet

1947 thriller *Dark Passage*.) This is the same spot to which we just directed the 'short trip' people.

Walk downhill on the steps right alongside the Bogey-Bacall building. As you descend, you'll see marvelous gardens and quaint cottages intermixed with more modern residences. You may even see—or more likely hear—the famed wild parrots of Telegraph Hill. Ahead are great views of Treasure Island and Oakland. This

View from the Filbert Steps

is the **Filbert Steps**, a dedicated city street, where generations of gardeners, led and inspired by the late Grace Marchant, made the rock of Telegraph Hill bloom.

About halfway down on your left, you'll see a sign for **Napier Lane**, a boardwalk that's also a city street. You're free to walk down this right-of-way as well as Filbert, but please respect the privacy of residents and don't go through gates or onto porches. Many of these houses were built in the 1860s and 1870s, clinging to the cliff that was left after the Bay-facing piece of Telegraph Hill was excavated to provide ballast for ships heading out of the Bay after disgorging their cargos, human and otherwise.

At the bottom of the steps, you'll find yourself on a little stub of Filbert Street. Walk straight ahead, crossing **Sansome Street**, and continue straight into **Levi's Plaza**, today's headquarters of the clothing company founded by Levi Strauss in the Gold Rush era. In the building to your right, you'll see a free company museum with fascinating displays.

When you're done looking, keep walking straight. You'll cross **Battery Street** and wind through a public park, contributed by Levi's to the city, to find yourself on **The Embarcadero** again. Look across the roadway toward the piers and you'll see the **Pier 23 café**, one of the last of the waterfront 'dives' that once served longshoremen and sailors when this was the maritime heart of the Pacific Coast. Drop in for a beer or a meal, and frequently jazz as well.

If you've had enough walking, board an F-line streetcar in either direction at the nearest stop, right in front of Pier 23.

If you're still game, stroll south toward the Ferry Building along the **Herb Caen Promenade** in front of the Pier buidings. You'll pass the Exploratorium at Pier 15, one of America's premier science experiences.

Shortly, you'll reach **Broadway,** where you'll see **Pier 7** jutting out into the Bay. It's a recreational pier for pedestrians with wonderful Bay views, well worth the detour. Continuing south, you'll reach **Pier 5**, with the historic Bay ferry *Santa Rosa* tied up alongside. The ferry is now the headquarters of Hornblower, which runs Bay cruises, but the uppermost deck is public open space you're allowed to enter during normal business hours. Don't be afraid; walk down the gangplank onto the ferry and follow the signs marked **Public Shore**.

From the ferryboat on Pier 5, follow the public walkways along the edge of the pier buildings. You'll see a large, handsome square structure sticking out from **Pier 3** on the Bay. Now a popular restaurant, from 1927 to 1941 this was the waiting room

Photo credit: Rick Laubscher.

for the steamboats *Delta Queen* and *Delta King,* which provided overnight service to Sacramento.

Returning to the promenade alongside The Embarcadero, you're now approaching the **Ferry Building**, which was once the second-busiest transit terminal in the world (behind London's Charing Cross). Opened in 1898, it lost its main purpose when the Bay Bridge opened in 1936. It slowly declined, a process accelerated when the State of California slapped a double-deck freeway directly in front of it in the late 1950s. Thirty years later, the 1989 earthquake crippled the freeway, which was removed to create the grand waterfront boulevard you see today, including the F-line.

The Ferry Building itself was completely renovated in 1998, its original interior skylights and iron framing uncovered and the interior opened up and converted to combine a local food marketplace and office space. Savor the wonderful harvest of Northern California in the food stalls open daily and at the outdoor farmers' market, one of California's best, on Tuesday and Saturday mornings.

From the Ferry Building, it's a short stroll across the street and a half block south to reach the **San Francisco Railway Museum**, where you can learn more about San Francisco's transit history.

The walk from Coit Tower to the Ferry Building is exactly one mile, and power walkers can cover it in 20 minutes, though you could easily spend half a day sauntering along this route.

2 Cable Cars, Chinatown Bars, and a Dead Detective

Start this walk by hopping off a **Powell Street cable car** at **Washington and Mason Streets,** or walk three blocks north (past the Fairmont Hotel) on Mason from the California cable line.

The **Cable Car Museum** (free admission) is your first stop (see description on page 73). After you've finished there, walk north along Mason Street past the front of the cable car barn. You'll see an entrance where you can get a glimpse of the cable car winding machinery and other aspects of the operation. Do not go in, however: this area is closed to the public.

Continue to **Jackson Street**. Here, you'll see one of the two places where cable cars cross. Mason Street cable cars headed downtown have to drop their cable and coast across this intersection because the crossing cable cars, headed for Hyde Street, have the upper cable (because they're headed uphill). If the Mason car didn't drop the cable, the grip would hit the Hyde line cable and do serious damage.

Head downhill on Jackson. You'll notice two cable car slots on this street but three rails. This is called a 'gauntlet track'. It's there because the Mason and

Gauntlet track on Jackson Street

From the Seat to Your Feet

Hyde lines diverge at the top of this block and both need a separate cable to pull them up the hill and onward. The cars share the center rail (obviously not at the same time). Around the corner on **Powell**, you'll see the dip in the pavement so the Mason and Hyde cars 'kneel down' to grasp their respective cables. Across the street at the track dip is the Chinatown branch of the San Francisco Public Library, built in 1921 and funded by Andrew Carnegie.

Actually, until 1958, this was known as the 'North Beach Branch Library'. The name change in part signals the expansion of what was traditionally known as Chinatown in San Francisco. Walk downhill on Jackson one block to **Stockton Street** and you'll see. When Muni's original F-line opened on Stockton in 1914, there were few Chinese businesses here. Today, Stockton is Chinatown's main shopping street; Grant Avenue is largely for tourists. Still, there are surprises on Grant, so walk another block downhill on Jackson, passing the 1925 Chinese Hospital, the only one of its kind in the U.S. (with a modern facility next door) and then **turn right on Grant**.

Rather than just looking at the store windows, turn your gaze upward to see some remnants of the old Chinatown on Grant Avenue, like the original neon sign of the Eastern Bakery at the corner of Commercial Street. Also, consider a peek into one of the two memorable dive bars on this

Interior of Li Po (the Buddha Lounge is just across the street)

block: Li Po on the left (try a mai tai if you dare) or the Buddha Lounge on the right at the corner of Washington.

A few steps downhill on **Washington** you'll see a bank built in a pagoda style, one of the few examples of authentic traditional Chinese architecture in Chinatown (most buildings are of western design and construction with pagoda roofs and balconies grafted on). This was the Chinese Telephone Exchange, built in 1909, where for decades young women would connect callers to other subscribers, by name, not number, in any of five Chinese dialects, and all from memory.

Continuing along **Grant Avenue** southward from Washington Street, **Commercial Street** will come up on the left in a half block. You can see the Ferry Building tower bracketed by the high-rises of Embarcadero Center. If you're headed that way, this is a pleasant stroll. Otherwise, continue on Grant a couple more blocks until you reach **California Street** and Old St. Mary's, California's

The old Chinese Telephone Exchange

Eastern Bakery and Republic Hotel, authentically old Chinatown

Sam Spade's partner Miles Archer was murdered by Brigid O'Shaughnessy.

Now follow Hammett's own footsteps to complete this walk. Backtrack those few steps and **walk down the stairway**. You're descending into the **Stockton Tunnel**, following the route Hammett might have taken from his apartment in the alley across Bush Street (Monroe, now renamed Dashiell Hammett) to reach his job as a copywriter at Samuel's Jewelers on Market Street. (Earlier, he was a Pinkerton detective in Suite 314 of the Flood Building.)

The Stockton Tunnel was built in 1914 primarily to provide a level route for Muni's original F-line to reach North Beach from Market Street. At the bottom of the stairs, walk south, away from the tunnel, and you'll reach **Union Square** in two blocks. Named for

first Catholic Cathedral, whose walls date to 1854.

If you've had enough walking, catch a California cable car headed downhill through the Financial District to Market Street, and then an F-line streetcar in either direction from there.

If you'd like to explore more on foot or are headed for the Union Square area, continue for two more blocks on Grant Avenue. When you reach the **Chinatown gate at Bush Street**, turn right up the hill one block, passing *Eglise Notre Dame des Victoires*, a gem of a church reflecting the early influence of French settlers in San Francisco. The congregation dates back to 1856; this iteration of the church was finished in 1915.

Cross Stockton Street and walk a few feet farther up Bush on the south sidewalk. You'll see a street sign saying *Burritt* and a plaque marking perhaps the most famous fictional crime scene in San Francisco, from the opening pages (and film frames) of Dashiell Hammett's *Maltese Falcon*, the spot where

Original F-line streetcar emerges from the Stockton Tunnel below Bush St., 1949

anti-secession rallies held here before the Civil War, it has been renovated several times in its history, most recently at the turn of the 21st century. Great people watching at any hour of the day here. You'll emerge at the corner of Powell and Geary, across from the St. Francis, one of San Francisco's most historic hotels. Follow the cable car tracks downhill and you'll reach **Market Street** and the F-line in three blocks.

Not counting the time you spend in the Cable Car Museum, bars or shops, this is about a one-hour walk.

3 A Mix of Maritime and Military History

This walk can be started from any of the Fisherman's Wharf terminals of Muni's vintage transit lines. As an optional extra at the beginning of the walk, from the F-line terminal at Jefferson and Jones, turn left on **Jefferson**. The next two blocks on the waterside contain most of the remaining maritime businesses at the Wharf. Cut over to the water at **Al Scoma Way**, which leads to one of the Wharf's most popular restaurants. If you're not eating, turn left before you get there and walk along the seawall where some of the remaining actual fishing boats tie up.

Wander along what's called **Fish Alley** until it ends, then turn left and get back to Jefferson Street. You'll see the Argonaut Hotel across the street, occupying the Haslett Warehouse, which, when built in 1907, was part of the then-largest fruit and vegetable cannery in the world. Inside is the visitor center for **San Francisco Maritime National Historical Park**,

San Francisco Maritime National Historical Park

with excellent displays recounting the days when the city was the undisputed maritime center of the Pacific Coast.

Across the street from the visitor center is the **Hyde Street Pier** with its collection of historic ships maintained by the National Park Service. A local favorite is the *Eureka*, a classic Bay ferryboat that served both the Golden Gate and Oakland runs in its day. From the pier, continue west (away from the Wharf) on Jefferson, passing the Dolphin and South End clubs, which have been fixtures in this area for more than a century. Here, Jefferson becomes a pedestrian promenade, with a visible (but unused) railroad track running along it.

To your left, up the hill through the park and past the Hyde Street cable car turntable, you'll see **Ghirardelli Square**, America's first true adaptive reuse of an industrial complex for retail use, carried out by William Matson Roth, scion of a shipping family, in the 1960s. Walk along one of the park pathways to reach this National Historic Landmark complex.

After exploring the Ghirardelli complex, which includes one of San Francisco's oldest buildings, the 1864 Pioneer Woolen Mill, make your way uphill on **Larkin Street** one block to **North Point**. You're now under the signature clock tower of Ghirardelli Square. Walk west along the brick façade and reflect that this area was once permeated with the smell of cocoa being turned into chocolate—and a lot of other smells, too, for this was one of the West Coast's key manufacturing and warehousing centers. In fact, on the next block, now occupied by the curved Fontana apartment towers, an enormous brick warehouse stood for nearly a century. Its demolition and replacement by these high rises stirred civic outrage and helped lead to height limits along the waterfront.

Original F-line streetcar and the lost Fontana Warehouse, Van Ness and North Point, c. 1951

North Point Street was long the route of Muni's original F-line, which opened in 1914, linking Downtown with Chinatown, North Beach, and the Marina District. It was converted to trolley buses (the 30-Stockton line) in 1951.

North Point ends just past the Fontana Apartments at **Van Ness Avenue**, where you'll be facing a massive retaining wall. This is the boundary of **Fort Mason**, a former U.S. Army post dating back to 1855. It is now a National Historic District and part of the **Golden Gate National Recreation Area**, administered by the National Park Service.

Turn left and walk uphill one block to **Bay Street**, then turn right. You'll immediately see big gates across a roadway entering the Fort. Walk in through the pedestrian gate. Handsome white houses are on your left—formerly officers' quarters, now private residences. Follow the curving roadway, noting the parallel grassy strip to your left. From 1914 until 1948 this was the right-of-way for Muni's H-line, a crosstown streetcar route that linked Fort Mason with Civic Center and the Mission District via Van Ness and Potrero Avenues.

When you reach the intersection of **Franklin Street**, look straight ahead. You'll see a large white building to the right, once Fort Mason's headquarters, now those of the National Park

unit. Across the street to the left, you'll see a small shelter: one of the H-line stops built by Muni, nearly identical to one that survives on the J-line at 21st Street.

Turn right before you reach the headquarters, and pass to the right of the old post chapel, heading uphill. You'll pass the old Officers' Club on your right, followed by a sequence of lavish (by Army standards) historic homes for top officers (now private residences) that once had commanding views of the city before foliage grew up to block it. On your left, you'll see the original Fort Mason headquarters and post hospital, dating back to the Civil War.

Original Fort Mason Headquarters area

Ahead, a garage marks the end of the road. Take the narrow sidewalk to the right, walking amid a riot of foliage that makes you think you're in a quiet country town, far from a major city. The sidewalk turns into stairs heading down. At the bottom, you reach a little picnic ground. Turn left to discover a preserved Civil War battery installed to defend San Francisco Bay from the Confederacy!

Walk past the cannon and follow the path around to the left. You'll reach an old military building converted to a youth hostel and a concrete road. Walk to the railing and you'll have a great view of **Fort Mason**

From the Seat to Your Feet

Civil War era cannon, Fort Mason

Center, now home to dozens of nonprofits, museums and performing arts groups located in the historic **Port of Embarkation**, where 1.65 million American soldiers boarded ships during World War II to cross the Pacific. This is the proposed terminal of the historic streetcar extension.

Now turn around and walk down the hill on the concrete road (officially McDowell Avenue) back toward Fisherman's Wharf. Looking over the ledge, you'll see the easternmost snippet of natural shoreline in San Francisco, called **Black Point**. Everything east of here around the city's Bay front has been filled, walled or otherwise altered. Look out across the bay for great views of **Alcatraz**. That little rectangular building on a small pier just in front of you is where prison boats transported prisoners to and from Alcatraz. The huge curving pier beyond is **Municipal Pier**, built in the 1930s as a make-work project. A walk out to its end provides great views of the Wharf and the Bay and a chance to see local crabbers and fishermen in action.

When you leave Municipal Pier, follow the quiet street ahead; it's actually the end of busy Van Ness Avenue. The big building on your right with the arched windows is a fire department emergency pumping station, which can suck salt water out of the Bay and into the hydrant system if an earthquake should disable freshwater supplies. Further along on the right, you'll see old railroad tracks emerging from a boarded up tunnel and crossing to your left. Planning is underway to extend historic streetcar service along Beach Street and through this tunnel to reach Fort Mason Center.

If you follow those old railroad tracks to your left, you'll approach a streamlined white building situated on your right. White towers resembling the points of an anchor stick out on its flanks and a rack of concrete bleachers sits below the building.

This is now the **Maritime Museum**, built in 1938 as another WPA project and recently

Maritime Museum and Ghirardelli Square from Municipal Pier

renovated. Inside, you'll find displays, ship models, and other artifacts, but many visitors end up entranced by the murals, terrazzo designs and other period art.

At the end of this promenade, you're next to the **Hyde Street cable car turntable** on your right, offering you a ride back Downtown. Two blocks farther along Jefferson is the **F-line terminal** at Jones Street.

If you take in the historic ships and Maritime Museum, allow half a day to truly enjoy this walk.

Photo credits: Rick Laubscher.

4 Cable car Castro, Hiking the Heights, and Meandering in the Mission

The starting point for this walk is the F-line terminal where **Castro, Market, and 17th Streets** come together. This neighborhood, which used to be called Eureka Valley, was developed by transit in the 1890s—specifically, the big white cable cars that ran from the Ferry Building all the way out Market Street to Castro, then turned south and over the Castro hill to Noe Valley beyond.

After the 1906 earthquake, the cable cars on Market were converted to electric streetcars, but the Castro hill was too steep for streetcars, so cable cars were retained on Castro between 18th and 26th Streets until 1941. The neighborhood got another shot of transit adrenaline in 1918, when Muni opened the **Twin Peaks Tunnel**, whose East Portal split Market Street just west of Castro (just to the right of where the gigantic rainbow flag sits today). The flag marks **Harvey Milk Plaza**, a memorial to America's first openly gay big-city elected official. The plaza also serves as an entrance to the Castro Street Station of Muni Metro, the streetcar (light rail) subway that runs under Market Street and was connected to the Twin Peaks Tunnel in the 1970s.

Walk downhill (south) on **Castro**, following the route of the old cable car into what many consider Gay America's Main Street. A few doors down, you'll see the landmark 1922 **Castro Theater**, designed by famed local architect Timothy Pflueger, which has survived as a single-screen cinema with its wonderful period interior intact. Cross 18th Street and its 33-line trolley buses. San Francisco has the most extensive trolley bus installation in the

Western Hemisphere; the 33-line was its first, in 1935. (A ride uphill (west) on the 33 will take you through a super-tight U-turn to get across the face of Twin Peaks

Castro Street

and over to Golden Gate Park, a ride well worth taking if you have the time.)

Continue south past 18th Street on Castro, which now begins an uphill slope. At 575 Castro, you'll see what was once Harvey Milk's combination business (a camera store) and campaign headquarters for his successful run for the Board of Supervisors in 1977.

Continue up Castro, which gets steeper. You'll notice numerous glorious Victorian homes, many in the Queen Anne style with round turrets. The homes in this area had started to deteriorate from age as families began leaving the neighborhood for the suburbs in the 1950s and 1960s. New residents, largely gay and lesbian, saw these homes as treasures and have revitalized the neighborhood in several ways.

At **Liberty Street**, turn left. Walk up a quiet block of beautifully preserved homes to **Noe Street**. To continue along Liberty, climb the staircase ahead, framed by Art Deco apartment buildings. It's another of San Francisco's many stair-streets, with gardens on either side within the street right-of-way. Another quiet block

From the Seat to Your Feet

Liberty Street Steps at Noe Street

takes you to **Sanchez Street**, with dramatic views of Downtown to your left. Stay on Liberty past Sanchez, catching glimpses of the great views as you head downhill. Cross Church and walk another half-block downhill on Liberty and you'll reach the streetcar tracks of the J-line. From here, you can walk another block and a half on Liberty to see a wonderful collection of 1870s and 1880s homes in the **Liberty Hill Historic District**, doubling back to the J-line tracks to catch your ride.

The F-line streetcars go to and from their home, the Cameron Beach streetcar facility at Geneva and San Jose Avenues, via the J-line. If you see an F-line streetcar on the J-line, by rule it is supposed to accept passengers, so wave it down at a marked stop for a great ride in either direction. Otherwise, take a J-Church line light rail vehicle heading north (downhill from Liberty). It winds along a twisty right-of-way through what were once people's backyards (the only way to get over the steep hill when the line was built in 1917), emerging at 20th Street and a spectacular vista: the greensward of **Dolores Park** falling away toward the Mission District, the historic Spanish Revival towers of Mission High School framing the foreground, and the entire skyline, including the Bay Bridge, spreading out behind.

If time is short, stay on the J-line, which will cross Market St. in six blocks and enter the subway, taking you to Union Square (Powell Station) or the Ferry Building (Embarcadero Station).

If you have more time and are up for hoofing it a bit further, get off the J-line car at **18th Street** and turn right (east). Walk one block to **Dolores Street**, bisected by palm trees. Turn left (north) and walk two blocks to **Mission Dolores**, founded by Junipero Serra in 1776. Tours are available; don't miss the gardens and graveyard, an island of serenity in a busy part of town.

After leaving Mission Dolores,

View from Liberty Street near Sanchez

stay on the west sidewalk, noting the two cottages at 214 and 220 Dolores, dating from the 1850s, are remarkably untouched by time. Two more blocks takes you to **Market Street**. Looming ahead atop its serpentine cliff is the enormous **U.S. Mint** (sorry, no tours or samples) and beneath it, the little rail yard where Market Street Railway has restored several streetcars and a cable car for Muni (it's not generally accessible to the public either; sorry). At **Dolores and Market**, you can grab an F-line streetcar back downtown.

From Market and Castro to the J-line at Liberty Street is 0.8 miles, but there's a lot of climbing. From 18th and Church to Market and Dolores is 0.6 miles of relatively flatter walking. Allow two hours for the long itinerary.

Photo credits: Rick Laubscher.

5 Bay to Breakers and Back via the Ghost Streetcars of Lands End

Okay, this ride involves only today's historic transit vehicles. But it covers some of the city's most historic transit routes and best scenery at the same time. Note, though, that it's the longest and most strenuous of the walks; wear good walking shoes and take your time.

5-line streetcar at City Hall, 1941

Start this ride on **Market Street**, anywhere from Main Street west to McAllister. Board a **5-Fulton** trolley coach (a rubber-tired vehicle with two poles on the roof connected to overhead wires) at a curb stop.

This line is one of the city's oldest, originating in 1883 as a cable car operating on this route as far west as Stanyan and Fulton, the northeast corner of Golden Gate Park. When you ride today, you'll pass through **Civic Center** soon after leaving Market Street at McAllister. This monumental collection of public buildings is dominated by the 1915 **City Hall** with the world's fifth largest dome. But don't forget to look to your left as you pass Larkin to see the classic façade of the **Asian Art Museum**, originally the city's Main Library, and to your right to see the historic **Earl Warren State of California**

Building between Larkin and Polk.

Continuing west, you climb a hill. At Steiner, a park known as **Alamo Square** is one block to your left. Walk uphill on Steiner one more block and you'll find the **'painted ladies'**, the row of colorful Victorian houses fronting the city skyline immortalized in literally millions of tourist photos. (You can reach them directly on the 21-Hayes trolley coach from Market Street.)

At Central Avenue, the bus jogs one block south to Fulton. The cable cars and streetcars in this line's historic past cut diagonally to Masonic Avenue through the newish shopping center here now. For 60 years, this was a maintenance and storage facility for the old Market Street Railway Company.

Heading west now on Fulton, you climb a hill and pass by the Jesuit-led **University of San Francisco** campus, capped by the stunning 1914 **St. Ignatius Church**, a dominant landmark of northwest San Francisco in an eclectic architectural style. Three

St. Ignatius Church, 1941: the pre-1906 cable car tracks on this stretch of the 5-line lasted until the end of the streetcar era in 1948

blocks farther west on Fulton, at Willard, your bus passes an imposing wooden mansion with Doric columns, built in 1904 by a lumber baron. In the late 1960s, this home was maintained by legendary rock band Jefferson Airplane. Its address, 2400 Fulton, became the name of a compilation album.

Golden Gate Park is now on your left. At Sixth Avenue, you reach what was the end of cable car service on this route. After the 1906 earthquake, the route was converted to streetcars as the 5-line and extended to Ocean Beach by 1911. (The Sixth Avenue stop is a good jumping off point to see such Golden Gate Park attractions as the De Young Museum, the Academy of Sciences, and the Conservatory of Flowers, just for starters. We recommend doing a web search for information on current exhibits.)

Continuing west through what San Franciscans call the 'Avenues', you'll eventually see the breakers of the **Pacific Ocean** ahead of you. The bus will turn right just short of the ocean. Get off at the terminal. From the 1920s to the 1960s, this was San Francisco's hometown amusement park, Playland at the Beach, served by the streetcars (and after 1948,

Playland-at-the-Beach in its glory days, 1941

buses) of the 5-line as well as Muni's B-Geary streetcars (later the 38-line bus).

Walk one block west to reach **Great Highway**, the boulevard fronting the Pacific Ocean. Walk along the sidewalk and begin a long climb up the hill past the historic **Cliff House**. Restaurants

on this site date back to 1858. Today's Cliff House is the National Park Service's modification of the 1909 version and offers meals and libations. Just past it uphill, you'll see the foundation of **Sutro Baths**, a grand Victorian recreation center with seven saltwater pools of various temperatures, destroyed by fire in 1966.

Just beyond these ruins is the site of the old Sutro streetcar shed, terminus of a route you're about to retrace on foot. Continue a little further uphill on the sidewalk to a parking lot marked **Merrie Way** and turn left until you reach its end. You'll see a visitors center with plenty of information. Now you're at the **Lands End Trail**, recently restored with help from our friends at the nonprofit Golden Gate National Parks Conservatory. This trail takes you along a quite historic right-of-way.

The Lands End Trail was originally the route of the Ferries & Cliff House steam train, which opened in 1886. The steam train was soon connected to a cable car line running from the Ferries, combining to offer service from bay to ocean. (Those cable cars were housed at today's cable car barn at Washington and Mason Streets, which is still emblazoned *Ferries & Cliff House Railway*.) Converted to electric streetcars as the 1-line in 1905, countless San Franciscans and visitors enjoyed the wonderfully scenic ride around Lands End with its stunning views of the (pre-bridge) Golden Gate until a massive landslide wiped out the tracks in 1925.

Along today's Lands End Trail, you'll find interpretative signage pointing you toward vistas, shipwrecks, and other sights. About a mile past its start, the trail splits. One branch quickly

Lands End station with sightseeing streetcar, about 1908. The scrub has been supplanted today by extensive vegetation (much of it non-native)

reaches the **California Palace of the Legion of Honor**, a notable museum in Lincoln Park. (Hint: you can shorten your trip by taking this branch of the trail and catching the 18-line bus at the museum, then transferring to the 38-line bus on Geary at 33rd Avenue headed downtown. It will take you to Market at Third Street.)

The other branch of the Lands End Trail continues east through **Lincoln Park** on the old streetcar right-of-way, with more great vistas, until it reaches the street called **El Camino Del Mar**. Walk a short block east (to the left from the trailhead) and then turn right (south) on **32nd Street**, a long block of picturesque homes. The first cross street is California, where you can board today's 1-California line, a trolley bus that will take you downtown.

The portion of today's **1-California** line between 33rd and Sixth Avenues was Muni's C-line streetcar from 1915 until 1949. The section on California Street between Presidio Avenue and Steiner Street was the western end of the California Street cable car line until it was cut back to Van Ness Avenue in 1954. The bus jogs one block north to Sacramento Street, then (in the eastbound direction) moves one more block north to Clay. The portion of today's 1-line bus on Clay between Leavenworth and Kearny Streets is the route of the first cable car line in the world, the Clay Street Hill Railroad, opened by Andrew Hallidie in 1873. Today, this stretch of Clay features the homes and businesses of Nob Hill and Chinatown. By staying on the 1-line bus, you'll retrace this route, and then jog through the **Financial District** to end up at Clay and Drumm Streets, near the Ferry Building. Or, you can get off the bus at Van Ness, walk two blocks south (to the right) and grab today's California Street cable car to finish your journey with a serene ride over Nob Hill.

The walking distance of this tour, from the end of the 5-line bus at Ocean Beach to the 1-line bus at 32nd and California, is 2.5 miles. Walking distance is 1.6 miles if you catch the 18-line bus at the California Palace of the Legion of Honor. Allow at least four hours—a full day if you take additional walks through Golden Gate Park.

Lands End Trail today

Gold Rush to Golden Era of Cable 1848-1906

First cable car line, Clay Street

Few cities grew up as fast as San Francisco. In 1848, the town held 1,000 people, but José de Jesús Noe's rancho around Twin Peaks had twice that many cattle. Within 25 years, though, San Francisco was America's tenth largest city, home to 150,000 people. Riches flowed to San Francisco from both the Gold Rush and Nevada's Comstock Lode, while its natural harbor made it a hub of commerce. Its extensive street grid, presciently laid out in 1847, included a 120-foot-wide main stem, Market Street, giving the new city room to grow.

A steam train on Market, opened in 1860, was the first public rail transit. It was soon supplanted by several horse-drawn street railways. But on the city's hills, horses struggled, a problem that inspired British mining engineer Andrew Hallidie to adapt his cable ore conveyors to pull rail cars. Hallidie's Clay Street Hill Railroad, opened in 1873, briefly revolutionized mass transit. Almost 30 U.S. cities, including New York, Chicago, Kansas City, Seattle, Los Angeles, and Oakland soon opened cable lines, which were twice as fast as horsecars, even on flat routes. In San Francisco, cable lines proliferated, helping create neighborhoods along Castro, California, Haight, Hayes, and many other streets while cementing Market Street, with its five cable lines, as the core commercial street.

Cable's national reign was fleeting. In 1887, Frank Sprague's electric streetcar in Richmond, VA sparked another revolution, again doubling transit speed and creating 'streetcar suburbs' out of empty land.

But San Francisco stayed attached to its cables for a combination of physical and political reasons. Five years into the 20th Century, when cable cars were considered obsolete almost everywhere else, they still ruled the roost in San Francisco, so dominant that an entire part of the city, 'South of the Slot', was known by its proximity to the cable channel running along Market Street.

Everything changed on the morning of April 18, 1906.

1776 Mission Dolores and the Presidio established by Spanish settlers

1847 Yerba Buena renamed San Francisco
Jasper O'Farrell designs street grid

1849 Gold Rush

1850 California becomes 31st state

1851 First public transit in San Francisco: horse-drawn omnibus between Portsmouth Square and Mission Dolores

1859 Comstock Lode silver strike in Nevada; riches flow to San Francisco for 15 years

1860 First rail transit in San Francisco: Market Street Railroad Co. operates steam train on Market and Valencia Streets

Pony Express connects San Francisco to the East

1864 San Francisco & San Jose Railroad completed (today's Caltrain)

1867 Steam operation banned on Market Street; horsecars take over

1869 Transcontinental Railroad completed, from Omaha, Nebraska to Sacramento

Becoming a Streetcar City 1892-1912

Metropolitan Railroad streetcar, circa 1892

Cable technology could only go so far, literally. Expensive to build and maintain, and slower than 10 miles per hour, cable lines were impractical beyond a few miles. So cable cars couldn't develop the western or southern halves of San Francisco. Heading for the Cliff House, for example, meant transferring to a steam train.

American transit was privately owned then. Operators paid cities for the right to put tracks in streets. In San Francisco, the all-powerful Southern Pacific Railroad was behind a consolidation of street railways in 1893. Most urban transit fares in America were regulated, generally at a nickel, so minimizing costs was critical to earning profits. This led companies to embrace electric streetcars across the country, since their variable costs were half those of cable cars, and several times cheaper than horsecars.

San Francisco's first streetcar line opened in 1892, near the San Francisco Railway Museum on Steuart Street, running nine miles to Daly's Hill (now Daly City), an unthinkable distance for a cable car. Soon several cable and horse lines around town were converted. By 1903, streetcars extended 20 miles south to San Mateo. But on Market Street, the backbone transit corridor, civic leaders opposed streetcars' overhead electric wires. They wanted the more expensive underground power conduits installed in Washington and New York, but the powerful transit company, United Railroads, resisted.

The earthquake and fire of April 18, 1906 turned San Francisco transit, like the rest of the town, upside down. Many cable facilities were destroyed or damaged. United Railroads, seeing an opportunity, won the 'temporary' right to erect overhead wires on Market, made permanent through bribery. Streetcars on Market moved people faster and helped accelerate the city's recovery. Despite the way it was done, the arrangement stood and the city's transit was transformed.

But not without lasting consequences.

1873 Andrew Hallidie's Clay Street Hill Railroad opens, the world's first commercially successful cable car operation

1876 Southern Pacific completes railroad between San Francisco and Los Angeles

1878 California Street Cable Railroad opens, portions of which remain in service today

1883 Market Street Cable Railway replaces horsecar line on Market & Valencia Streets; Park & Ocean Railroad opens, with steam trains linking Haight & Stanyan to Ocean Beach via H Street (now Lincoln Way)

1887 Frank Sprague inaugurates first practical electric streetcar in Richmond, Virginia, supplanting cable cars as 'state-of-the-art' transit technology

1888 Powell Street Railway Company opens cable lines on Powell, Mason, Washington, and Jackson Streets; portions remain in service today

Steam train opens from Central (Presidio Ave.) & California to Cliff House via Land's End

1891 O'Farrell, Jones & Hyde cable car line opens; most of Hyde Street segment remains in service today

City bans overhead trolley wires from downtown, specifically Market Street

1892 City's first electric railways open, including San Francisco & San Mateo Electric Railroad Company, with terminal on Steuart Street near Market Street

1893 Southern Pacific interests create Market Street Railway, consolidating many smaller companies; begins converting many horse-drawn and cable lines to electric streetcars

1898 New Ferry Building completed at the foot of Market Street

Birth of Muni: New infrastructure for the new century 1912-1928

Muni opens, December 28, 1912

The combination of bribery and a bitter 1907 strike made United Railroads unpopular in San Francisco. Meanwhile in 1909, after twice rejecting the idea, San Francisco voters approved city purchase of the Geary Street cable line and its conversion to electric streetcars. On December 28, 1912, the first publicly–owned big city transit line in America opened. An astonishing 50,000 San Franciscans showed up at Geary & Market to hear Mayor James Rolph call the Geary line "the people's road... the nucleus of a mighty system of streetcar lines which will someday encompass the entire city." He then personally piloted the first streetcar (preserved car No. 1) of the Municipal Railway.

City Chief Engineer Michael M. O'Shaughnessy largely fulfilled Rolph's promises. Working from noted transit consultant Bion Arnold's plan, the 'Chief' built quickly to serve the throngs expected for the 1915 Panama-Pacific International Exposition, which San Franciscans saw as a celebration of the city's rebirth. Just over two years after its opening day,

Muni had added five permanent lines, including the original F-line, using a new tunnel on Stockton between Union Square and Chinatown to reach the exposition in today's Marina District.

Muni then switched focus, opening the J-Church line into the Mission District in 1917 and penetrating the western half of the city the following year via the Twin Peaks Tunnel, funded by property owners to develop new neighborhoods. United Railroads badly wanted access to the tunnel, but Mayor Rolph prevailed, reserving the tunnel exclusively for Muni. The K, L, and M lines fanned out from West Portal, spurring new homebuilding; then in 1928, Muni opened the N-Judah line through the new Sunset Tunnel, west to Ocean Beach. These Muni lines spurred the development of what was then the 'empty quarter' of San Francisco.

Though O'Shaughnessy's biggest engineering achievement was the city's monumental water and power system, his Muni legacy remains the most visible to San Franciscans.

1902

Market Street Railway Company acquired by Brown Brothers of New York, consolidated with San Francisco & San Mateo Electric Railroad and Sutter Street Railroad to form United Railroads of San Francisco

1903

Bond issue to buy Geary St. cable line and convert to city-owned streetcars fails for second time

United Railroads opens electric streetcar service between downtown San Francisco and San Mateo, 20 miles south

1905

Lands End steam train converted to electric streetcars serving Cliff House and Sutro Baths

1906

Earthquake and fire devastate San Francisco

Aided by bribes, United Railroads wins permission to convert Market Street cable car lines to electric streetcars, which aid significantly in reconstruction

1907

Bitter strike by United Railroads car men; key issue is eight-hour day

1909

San Francisco voters approve bonds to acquire Geary cable car line, convert it to electric streetcar with overhead wires, and extend the line to the Ferry Building via Market Street

1912

Municipal Railway of San Francisco (Muni) opens December 28 on Geary Street

Mayor James Rolph operates first streetcar (car No. 1); promises 'great municipal system'

1913

Geary Street Muni lines extended to Ferry Building and Ocean Beach; landmark study recommends aggressive expansion of Muni system

Muni takes over Presidio & Ferries Railroad on Union

Last horsecar runs in San Francisco

1914

Spurred by 1915 Panama-Pacific Int'l Exposition, Muni expands; builds Stockton Tunnel to serve Expo

U.S. Army extends State Belt waterfront freight trackage through tunnel under Fort Mason to Presidio; line helps build Exposition

1915

Panama-Pacific world's fair attracts millions; Muni and United Railroads streetcars handle bulk of visitors, clearly establishing San Francisco as a 'streetcar city'

Jitneys provide stiff competition for the first time

The Roar of the Four: Market Street 1918-1948

Market Street at Geary, circa 1938

The 1898 Ferry Building served as San Francisco's 'front door' for half a century; Market Street was its spine. By 1913, a dozen United Railroads streetcar lines served Market Street, and the newly-formed San Francisco Municipal Railway wanted a piece of Market Street too. The solution was to lay down another pair of tracks for Muni, placed outside the United Railroads tracks from the Ferry Building to Castro Street. By 1918, eight Muni lines used those tracks, making Market Street, along with New Orleans' Canal Street, the only U.S. main streets with such a four-track arrangement.

In the 1920s, San Francisco's landmark Ferry Building was the busiest transportation terminal in America—behind only London's Charing Cross Station worldwide—with more than 800 streetcars swinging through the triple loop in the 90-minute evening rush hour to serve the 43 ferryboats that tied up there. At stops along Market, barely two feet separated streetcars on the inside and outside tracks, forcing passengers waiting for cars on the inside tracks to squeeze sideways as cars rumbled by.

People from all around the Bay Area came to Market Street to shop at department stores like the Emporium, Hale's, and Weinstein's. They came to see movies at the Warfield, the State, and the grandest of all, the Fox. They came to visit their doctors and dentists at the Flood Building, and for dozens of other reasons. Market Street was one of the busiest streets in the world.

The opening of the San Francisco-Oakland Bay Bridge in 1936 changed the scene. More automobiles descended on the city. When interurban trains began running on the bridge in 1939, ferry traffic declined further and many streetcars were diverted to the Transbay Terminal at First & Mission Streets. World War II rejuvenated Market Street and its streetcars as soldiers and sailors shipped in and out, but soon after the War ended, so did the fabled 'Roar of the Four'.

1917
Muni opens J-Church line through Mission district

Another strike hits United Railroads

1918
Muni opens world's longest streetcar tunnel from Castro & Market under Twin Peaks

Streetcar crash kills 8, worst SF transit accident ever

Muni opens first motorbus line across Golden Gate Park

1919
Muni's L-Taraval streetcar line opens as shuttle running westward from West Portal, extended four years later through Twin Peaks Tunnel to Ferry Building

1921
Financially weakened United Railroads emerges as Market Street Railway Co. due to bondholder foreclosure

1925
Landslide closes 1-Cliff streetcar line around Lands End; portions of right-of-way are today a hiking trail in Golden Gate National Recreational Area

Muni opens M-line as a streetcar shuttle from West Portal to Ocean View

1920s
Ferry Building is busiest transit terminal in America (behind only London's Charing Cross worldwide); up to 800 streetcars per hour use triple track loop at Ferry Building and four tracks on Market Street

1926
Market Street Railway Company adopts famed, easy-to-see 'White Front' paint scheme for its vehicles

1927
Steamboats *Delta King* and *Delta Queen* begin overnight service between San Francisco's Pier 3 and Sacramento

1928
Muni builds Sunset Tunnel under Buena Vista Park, opens N-Judah streetcar line

1929
Pacific Avenue cable car line closes

Depression, War, Consolidation, and Conversion 1935-1951

Market Street Railway Co. home-built 'White Front' car

Muni's private competitor had reclaimed the name Market Street Railway Company in 1921. The city wanted to take it over but voters repeatedly rejected the idea. Market Street Railway Co. ran on a shoestring to stay in business, operated first by a utility management company named Byllesby, and later by Samuel Kahn, who acquired the railway. The company built 250 of its own streetcars (of which preserved No. 798 is the sole survivor) and bought others secondhand to save money. To gain more visibility, the ends of its vehicles were painted bright white, in contrast to Muni's gray.

In 1935, Market Street Railway Co. won a court case overturning a city ordinance requiring two crew members per streetcar. This cut costs for the struggling company, but the decision was reversed in 1939. The company had already converted the lightly patronized 33-line over Twin Peaks into San Francisco's first trolley bus route; now it started supplanting other streetcar routes, including Third and Polk Streets, with single–operator buses, and raised fares from 5 to 7 cents, which drove more riders to Muni.

World War II stopped production of transit vehicles, and gasoline rationing jammed transit with riders, wearing out both streetcars and track. In 1944, San Francisco voters finally approved Muni's takeover of Market Street Railway Company. The first plan called for retaining 14 streetcar lines, including those on Mission, Sutter, Stockton, and Union Streets, as well as the San Mateo interurban, but after voters approved a bond issue in 1947, the focus changed. By 1951, only seven streetcar lines survived, all originally Muni's. The 'White Front' cars of Market Street Railway Co. were history, replaced by the most extensive trolley bus system in the U.S., powered by the O'Shaughnessy–built Hetch Hetchy hydroelectric system in Yosemite. Even the J-Church was slated to convert to trolley buses until Noe Valley residents rose up in opposition. Rail transit in San Francisco was under siege.

1932

Height of rail transit service in SF, with more than 50 streetcar lines and seven cable car lines

Market Street Railway Co. opens 31-Balboa 'high speed' line, last new streetcar line for 63 years

1933

Last streetcar to be built in San Francisco by Market Street Railway Company workers (car No. 994) completed at site of today's Muni Green Division

Coit Tower completed

1934

Market Street Railway Company employees unionize; company wins ruling to operate cars with single-person crew; 18 lines converted to this standard

Alcatraz becomes federal prison

General Strike cripples city

1935

Market Street Railway Co. converts 33-line across Twin Peaks to first trolley bus line in SF

Pan Am inaugurates China Clipper air passenger service between San Francisco and Hawaii

1936

Bay Bridge opens to motor vehicles

Revolutionary PCC streetcar enters service in Pittsburgh and Brooklyn; designed to compete with automobiles and buses, ultimately 33 cities will use what becomes the most successful U.S. streetcar ever

1937

Golden Gate Bridge opens

1938

Market Street Railway Company ordered to return to two-person crews on all streetcars; 19-Polk is first streetcar line to be converted to buses the following year

1939

Treasure Island World's Fair

Transbay Terminal serves Bay Bridge interurban trains from as far as Chico

Ferry Building traffic rapidly diminishes

Muni buys 'Magic Carpet' streetcars, resembling PCCs

1941

Market Street Railway Company cutbacks: Castro cable line closed; counterbalance (cable-aided) streetcars on Fillmore St. Hill in Marina closed; streetcar lines serving Bayview district on Third Street abandoned, restored 65 years later as Muni's T-line

1942

Sacramento-Clay cable car line, incorporating world's first cable car route, closes

World War II gas rationing and conservation measures drive up streetcar ridership and forestall further rail-to-bus conversions

The Cable Car Wars 1947-1954

Cable car protest, 1954

By the 1940s, motor bus improvements let them climb almost any hill. Market Street Railway Company converted its Castro cable car line to buses in 1941, followed by Sacramento-Clay in 1942, but World War II postponed possible conversion of the Powell-Mason and Washington-Jackson lines. After Muni's takeover, Mayor Roger Lapham advocated buses for those two lines.

"Not so fast," said Friedel Klussmann, arguing the cable cars were a symbol of the city. The political and business ruling class—exclusively male—derided her. With no campaign experience, she got a measure on the ballot and rallied voters to crush Lapham's plan by a margin of 3 to 1, saving the two cable car lines.

In 1951, the California Street Cable Railroad Company, which also ran lines on O'Farrell, Jones, and Hyde Streets, went out of business after 74 years. Pro-cable forces got the city to buy it in 1952, but city voters turned down a bond issue to rehabilitate its lines in 1953. Downtown interests,

seeking more one-way streets for automobiles, took aim at the 'Cal Cable' lines.

Attorney Morris Lowenthal led the opposition this time, Friedel Klussman joining in later. A deal was almost struck to keep all the trackage except that on O'Farrell Street, but Klussmann said no. Another plan, to combine the inner end of the California Street line and the outer end of the Hyde Street line, gave way to a more radical ballot proposal cutting off the scenic Pacific Heights portion of the Washington-Jackson line and combining it with the Hyde Street trackage to form a 'new' Powell-Hyde line—meanwhile cutting the California Street line in half to dead-end at Van Ness Avenue. Muni's governing commission secretly hired a PR man to set up a fake citizens committee that misled many voters into thinking they were saving the cable cars when, in fact, they were greatly reducing the system. The proposal passed at the polls, creating the three-line cable car system we ride today.

1944

After six defeats beginning in 1925, San Francisco voters approve city purchase of Market Street Railway Company; its operations are merged with Muni's on September 29

1946

Muni begins removal of outer set of streetcar tracks on Market Street, ending—two years later—the era of complete streetcar supremacy on its main street known as the Roar of the Four

1947

SF voters overwhelmingly rally behind activist Friedel Klussmann and reject Mayor Roger Lapham's proposal to convert Powell cable car lines to buses; but voters also approve bond issue to overhaul transit infrastructure

1948

Muni takes delivery of its first true PCC streamliner streetcars; ten double-end cars join the five look-alike Magic Carpets

1949

Last streetcar service to Ferry Building ends

40-line interurban streetcar service to San Mateo discontinued

1951

F-Stockton streetcar is converted to trolley bus (30-Stockton), ending a three-year changeover that saw two dozen San Francisco streetcar lines disappear

1952

Muni begins operating cable car lines on California, Hyde, and Jones streets, acquired from bankrupt California Street Cable Railroad

1954

Following intense civic battle, SF voters narrowly agree to a 'consolidation' of cable car system, cutting its route mileage in half and eliminating all service west of Van Ness Avenue

1956

Muni's first streetcar line, on Geary Street, is converted to buses (38-Geary)

Washington & Jackson cable car line closes

1957

First 'new' cable car line in 63 years opens, Powell-Hyde combines parts of old Washington-Jackson and O'Farrell, Jones & Hyde lines

Last remaining street-running cable car outside San Francisco closes in Dunedin, New Zealand

Near Death for Streetcars 1951-1982

Last day of the 5-McAllister streetcar, 1948

After World War II, Americans migrated to new suburbs—with no mass transit. Now automobile-dependent, suburban drivers commuting to the cities wanted more parking and traffic lanes. Combined with worn-out transit infrastructure and the actions of bus and petroleum interests, this trend doomed dozens of streetcar systems nationwide. Even the streamlined 'PCC', widely considered the best streetcar ever designed (by the Presidents' Conference Committee of U.S. transit executives in the 1930s) couldn't stem the tide in most of the 33 cities that ran it, despite the fact that it cut labor costs by only requiring one operator.

Muni bought five PCC-like cars in 1939, ten actual PCCs in 1948, and ordered the last 25 PCCs to be built in the United States in 1951. But it gained no immediate labor savings because voters in union-proud San Francisco kept saying 'no' to one-operator streetcars. Running budget deficits by this time, Muni responded by replacing all streetcar service west of the Twin Peaks Tunnel with buses

nights and Sundays.

In 1954, voters finally changed their minds, but only for PCCs. Muni wanted to buy more, but lacked capital funding, so many of Muni's boxy original streetcars stayed in service and became known as 'Iron Monsters'. But Mack offered Muni diesel buses in an affordable lease arrangement, and in 1956, Muni converted its first (and busiest) line, the B-Geary, from streetcars to buses. The next year, Muni managed to lease used PCCs (from St. Louis) and added 70 cars to replace the remaining 'Iron Monsters' on the five surviving streetcar lines.

In 1962, voters approved the Bay Area Rapid Transit District (BART), including a two-level subway under Market Street: one for BART trains, one for Muni streetcars. After seemingly endless planning and discussion, Muni purchased new 'light rail vehicles' (LRVs) from Boeing to operate in the subway, continuing on the surface along the outer ends of the J, K, L, M, and N lines. In the fall of 1982, surface rail transit on Market ended after 122 years. Or so it seemed.

1958

Last original-style Muni streetcars
retired, only PCC streetcars remain

Key System trains on Bay Bridge replaced by buses

Last old-style ferryboat to Ferry Building discontinued

Giants move to SF

1959

Double-deck Embarcadero Freeway opens;
visually cuts off Ferry Building from Market St.

1962

Voters in three counties
approve Bay Area Rapid Transit
District (BART) construction bonds

1963

Fox Theater at 9th & Market
Streets, San Francisco's greatest
movie house, demolished

Alcatraz federal prison closes

1964

Cable cars declared
U.S. National Historic Landmark

1965

Women allowed to ride on
cable car outer steps for first time

1966

Sutro Baths, transit destination
for generations, destroyed by fire

1967

Construction begins on Market
Street Subway, with two levels,
one for BART, one for Muni streetcars

1974

BART begins regular transbay
service in Market Street subway

Muni introduces Fast Pass monthly fare card

1978

Mayor George Moscone and Supervisor
Harvey Milk assassinated at City Hall;
Dianne Feinstein becomes mayor

Rebirth of Vintage Streetcars and Market Street Railway 1983-present

1984 Trolley Festival opening day

Streetcars survived in San Francisco because Muni's tunnels couldn't easily be adapted for buses. Because of BART, Muni got a streetcar subway and modern cars. A related Market Street 'beautification' scheme planned to eliminate the overhead transit wires originally put there by bribery in 1906, but citizens wanted to keep non–polluting electric trolley buses, so the wires stayed. As for traditional streetcars, Muni planners proposed two 'vintage' lines around 1980: the E-Embarcadero, using the abandoned State Belt freight railroad alignment to Fort Mason, and the F-Market, from the Ferry Building to Castro. These plans initially attracted little interest.

Then in 1982, the entire cable car system—by now decrepit and dangerous—was shut down for total rebuilding. Concerned about tourism, the Chamber of Commerce approached Mayor Dianne Feinstein with an idea for an 'Historic Trolley Festival' on Market for summer 1983. It was a huge hit. Riders loved the English 'Boat Tram' and the breezy Melbourne tram, as well as Muni's venerable car No. 1 from 1912, and even recently–retired streamliner PCCs.

Spurred by success, Mayor Feinstein brought the Trolley Festivals back for four more summers, while plans progressed for a permanent F-line, to be extended along The Embarcadero to Fisherman's Wharf.

The Chamber of Commerce turned over its supporting role to a small nonprofit group named for the original Market Street Railway Company, which quickly grew to more than 1,200 members and helped Muni acquire and restore additional vintage streetcars. F-line service opened on Market Street in 1995 and was extended to Fisherman's Wharf in 2000. With the boom along the waterfront, the E-line opened for daily service in 2016. Today Market Street Railway proudly supports Muni in its preservation and operation of vintage streetcars and cable cars, and welcomes your generous contributions to help us in our work. Visit streetcar.org for more information.

1979 Muni first proposes E-Embarcadero line from Fort Mason to the Peninsula train depot, using vintage streetcars; F-Market line is proposed the following year

1980 Muni Metro subway inaugurated under Market Street with N-Judah line

Caltrans assumes responsibility from Southern Pacific for the 117-year-old Peninsula commuter rail service, later to be run as Caltrain

1982 Cable car system shut down for complete rebuilding

Full-time Muni Metro subway operation commences

Market Street loses surface rail transit service for first time in 122 years

1983 Vintage streetcars return to Market Street for summer-long Historic Trolley Festival as alternate attraction for shutdown cable car system and demonstration project for F-line

1984 Rebuilt cable car system reopens

Trolley Festival operates a 2nd summer season at Mayor Feinstein's request, to growing public acclaim; festivals end in 1987 to rebuild tracks for permanent F-line

1985 Nonprofit group named for old Market Street Railway Company takes up support role for Trolley Festivals; leads call for permanent vintage streetcar service

1989 Loma Prieta earthquake hits, dooming double-deck Embarcadero Freeway; grand surface waterfront boulevard plan, already in development, extended to replace footprint of freeway; includes tracks for vintage streetcars

1993 After decades of declining waterfront freight traffic, last remnant of State Belt Railroad, now owned by city, is abandoned

1995 F-line opens from Castro to Transbay Terminal, reviving tradition of rail transit on Market Street; is first new streetcar line in SF in 63 years

2000 F-line extended to Fisherman's Wharf

2007 Streetcar service returns to Third Street for first time in more than 60 years

Trainspotter's Guide

1
☐ I saw this car!
☐ I rode this car! Date _____

130
☐ I saw this car!
☐ I rode this car! Date _____

162
☐ I saw this car!
☐ I rode this car! Date _____

578
☐ I saw this car!
☐ I rode this car! Date _____

798
☐ I saw this car!
☐ I rode this car! Date _____

C-1
☐ I saw this car! Date _____

189
☐ I saw this car!
☐ I rode this car! Date _____

228
☐ I saw this car!
☐ I rode this car! Date _____

233
☐ I saw this car!
☐ I rode this car! Date _____

351
☐ I saw this car!
☐ I rode this car! Date _____

496
☐ I saw this car!
☐ I rode this car! Date _____

578-J
☐ I saw this car!
☐ I rode this car! Date _____

737
☐ I saw this car!
☐ I rode this car! Date _____

913
☐ I saw this car!
☐ I rode this car! Date _____

916
☐ I saw this car!
☐ I rode this car! Date _____

952

☐ I saw this car!
☐ I rode this car! Date _____

1807

☐ I saw this car!
☐ I rode this car! Date _____

1811

☐ I saw this car!
☐ I rode this car! Date _____

1814

☐ I saw this car!
☐ I rode this car! Date _____

1815

☐ I saw this car!
☐ I rode this car! Date _____

1818

☐ I saw this car!
☐ I rode this car! Date _____

1856

☐ I saw this car!
☐ I rode this car! Date _____

1859

☐ I saw this car!
☐ I rode this car! Date _____

1888

☐ I saw this car!
☐ I rode this car! Date _____

1893

☐ I saw this car!
☐ I rode this car! Date _____

1895

☐ I saw this car!
☐ I rode this car! Date _____

1006

☐ I saw this car!
☐ I rode this car! Date _____

1007

☐ I saw this car!
☐ I rode this car! Date _____

1008

☐ I saw this car!
☐ I rode this car! Date _____

1009

☐ I saw this car!
☐ I rode this car! Date _____

Trainspotter's Guide

1010
- ☐ I saw this car!
- ☐ I rode this car! Date _____

1011
- ☐ I saw this car!
- ☐ I rode this car! Date _____

1015
- ☐ I saw this car!
- ☐ I rode this car! Date _____

1040
- ☐ I saw this car!
- ☐ I rode this car! Date _____

1050
- ☐ I saw this car!
- ☐ I rode this car! Date _____

1051
- ☐ I saw this car!
- ☐ I rode this car! Date _____

1052
- ☐ I saw this car!
- ☐ I rode this car! Date _____

1053
- ☐ I saw this car!
- ☐ I rode this car! Date _____

1055
- ☐ I saw this car!
- ☐ I rode this car! Date _____

1056
- ☐ I saw this car!
- ☐ I rode this car! Date _____

1057
- ☐ I saw this car!
- ☐ I rode this car! Date _____

1058
- ☐ I saw this car!
- ☐ I rode this car! Date _____

1059
- ☐ I saw this car!
- ☐ I rode this car! Date _____

1060
- ☐ I saw this car!
- ☐ I rode this car! Date _____

1061
- ☐ I saw this car!
- ☐ I rode this car! Date _____

1062
☐ I saw this car!
☐ I rode this car! Date _____

1063
☐ I saw this car!
☐ I rode this car! Date _____

1070
☐ I saw this car!
☐ I rode this car! Date _____

1071
☐ I saw this car!
☐ I rode this car! Date _____

1072
☐ I saw this car!
☐ I rode this car! Date _____

1073
☐ I saw this car!
☐ I rode this car! Date _____

1074
☐ I saw this car!
☐ I rode this car! Date _____

1075
☐ I saw this car!
☐ I rode this car! Date _____

1076
☐ I saw this car!
☐ I rode this car! Date _____

1077
☐ I saw this car!
☐ I rode this car! Date _____

1078
☐ I saw this car!
☐ I rode this car! Date _____

1079
☐ I saw this car!
☐ I rode this car! Date _____

1080
☐ I saw this car!
☐ I rode this car! Date _____

CABLE CARS

1
☐ I saw this car!
☐ I rode this car!   Date _____

2
☐ I saw this car!
☐ I rode this car!   Date _____

3
☐ I saw this car!
☐ I rode this car!   Date _____

4
☐ I saw this car!
☐ I rode this car!   Date _____

5
☐ I saw this car!
☐ I rode this car!   Date _____

6
☐ I saw this car!
☐ I rode this car!   Date _____

7
☐ I saw this car!
☐ I rode this car!   Date _____

9
☐ I saw this car!
☐ I rode this car!   Date _____

10
☐ I saw this car!
☐ I rode this car!   Date _____

11
☐ I saw this car!
☐ I rode this car!   Date _____

12
☐ I saw this car!
☐ I rode this car!   Date _____

13
☐ I saw this car!
☐ I rode this car!   Date _____

14
☐ I saw this car!
☐ I rode this car!   Date _____

15
☐ I saw this car!
☐ I rode this car!   Date _____

16
- [ ] I saw this car!
- [ ] I rode this car! Date _____

17
- [ ] I saw this car!
- [ ] I rode this car! Date _____

18
- [ ] I saw this car!
- [ ] I rode this car! Date _____

19
- [ ] I saw this car!
- [ ] I rode this car! Date _____

20
- [ ] I saw this car!
- [ ] I rode this car! Date _____

21
- [ ] I saw this car!
- [ ] I rode this car! Date _____

22
- [ ] I saw this car!
- [ ] I rode this car! Date _____

23
- [ ] I saw this car!
- [ ] I rode this car! Date _____

24
- [ ] I saw this car!
- [ ] I rode this car! Date _____

25
- [ ] I saw this car!
- [ ] I rode this car! Date _____

26
- [ ] I saw this car!
- [ ] I rode this car! Date _____

27
- [ ] I saw this car!
- [ ] I rode this car! Date _____

28
- [ ] I saw this car!
- [ ] I rode this car! Date _____

42
- [ ] I saw this car!
- [ ] I rode this car! Date _____

44 GIANTS
- [ ] I saw this car! Date _____

49 ☐ I saw this car!
☐ I rode this car! Date _____

50 ☐ I saw this car!
☐ I rode this car! Date _____

51 ☐ I saw this car!
☐ I rode this car! Date _____

52 ☐ I saw this car!
☐ I rode this car! Date _____

53 ☐ I saw this car!
☐ I rode this car! Date _____

54 ☐ I saw this car!
☐ I rode this car! Date _____

56 ☐ I saw this car!
☐ I rode this car! Date _____

57 ☐ I saw this car!
☐ I rode this car! Date _____

58 ☐ I saw this car!
☐ I rode this car! Date _____

59 ☐ I saw this car!
☐ I rode this car! Date _____

60 ☐ I saw this car!
☐ I rode this car! Date _____

VISIT THE
SAN FRANCISCO RAILWAY MUSEUM

San Francisco is one of the few places in the world where you can get the actual experience of riding vintage rail transit in its 'natural habitat'—the rumble of the motors under your feet, the swaying of the car itself, the smell of the brakes. Before or after you take that magical ride on these 'museums in motion', visit the free San Francisco Railway Museum to make your experience complete.

Located at the F-line Steuart Street stop, just across from the Ferry Building, the museum offers a celebration of San Francisco's rail transit history, focused on exploring the positive impacts streetcars and cable cars have made on the quality of urban life in this great city.

It features a full-sized exact replica of the motorman's platform of a 1911 San Francisco streetcar, where kids of all ages can experience what it was like to be at the controls. You'll also find unique historic artifacts, illustrative and informative displays, rarely seen archival photography, and audio-visual exhibits that use 21st century technology to bring rail transit in the 19th and 20th centuries to life.

The museum gift shop features a wide variety of unique San Francisco gifts, souvenirs and memorabilia not available anywhere else.

Open 10am-5pm daily. Closed Mondays.
For more information, call 415-974-1948.

www.streetcar.org/museum

ABOUT THE AUTHOR

Rick Laubscher is a fourth-generation San
Franciscan who fell in love with streetcars as a
child when his mother took him downtown on an
'iron monster' through the Twin Peaks Tunnel to
see the circus. He worked as a broadcast reporter in
San Francisco, then as a corporate executive, where
he began his advocacy for vintage streetcar service.
He now operates his own strategic communications
consultancy, Messagesmith, and serves as president
of the nonprofit Market Street Railway.